Modern Energy Tapping

Silvia Hartmann

First Edition
May 2018

Published By

DragonRising

www.DragonRising.com

Modern Energy Tapping
Bringing The Power Of The Positives Into YOUR Life!

© Silvia Hartmann 2018

First Edition 2018

ISBN (Paperback): 978-1-873483-96-1

Published by:

> DragonRising Publishing
> United Kingdom

> DragonRising.com

Other titles by this author:

> EMO Energy In Motion

> Infinite Creativity

> The Energy Symbols

> Modern Meditations

Printed and bound by CPI Group (UK) Ltd, Croydon, CR0 4YY

Table of Contents

Part 1 - Welcome To Modern Energy Tapping!

"There is only energy, and the absence of energy."
Silvia Hartmann

What is Modern Energy Tapping?

Modern Energy Tapping refers to using a simple sequence of energy points to make changes in the energy body.

Modern Energy Tapping follows the principles of Modern Energy Theory.

Modern Energy Tapping is not a psychology technique, it is an energy body centred approach to improve the conditions in the energy body.

Modern Energy Tapping is a method from The Third Field in the Mind, Body, Spirit (Energy Body) triad.

Modern Energy Tapping, or MET for short, relies on working with positive energy to energize, heal and re-charge the energy body.

Modern

New, not based on ancient systems or religions[1]

Energy

Energy body focused

Tapping

Lightly touching the energy body with the energy hands

---

1   The Principles of Modern Energy can be found in EMO Energy In Motion, Hartmann 2002/2011.

The Living Energy Body

Every person has a real energy body, whether they know this or not.

The energy body transmits its states of being through the medium of EMOTIONS.

Emotions range from fine sensations, also known as intuition, through all the various manifestations of emotions all the way to the high end emotions, known as psychosomatic emotions, which are indistinguishable from physical pain.

- ✖ Modern Energy Tapping does not treat physical problems.
- ✖ Modern Energy Tapping does not treat psychological problems.
- ✔ Modern Energy Tapping only treats energy body problems.

At first glance, this may not seem as important as physical or psychological problems.

However, there are many problems that cannot be solved in any other way than by treating the energy body.

Many more problems have an energy component which can influence the severity of the problems.

The energy body is essential
for well-being
in mind, body and spirit.

The 6th Sense

Our true 6th Sense are our emotions.

> ✳ Emotions are feedback from the energy body through the physical body.

> ✳ The energy body creates sensations that have no physical origin.

> ✳ Our emotional state tells us how our energy body is doing.

When we are happy, in love, feel strong and capable, our energy body is doing well. A lot of energy flows in, through and out the energy body, keeping it fresh and constantly energized.

When we are scared, upset, feel powerless and depressed, our energy body is not doing well. Energy is stuck, blocked, and we have no energy to deal with life.

People did not understand the connection between emotions and the energy body, and did not give any attention to the many "cries for help" the stressed energy body produces all the time.

Modern Energy, of which Modern Energy Tapping is an example and a good introduction, focuses on the energy body exclusively, because we now know that when we feed the energy body, not only do our emotions settle down, but we can also think much more clearly and our bodies become stronger.

By directly addressing the needs of the energy body, we have a simple, direct path to feeling better, thinking better, and becoming fitter and healthier.

The Energy Body Stress Factor

Everyone talks about stress, and everyone knows that when you get stressed, you start doing, feeling and thinking things you would never be doing, feeling or thinking on a "good day."

Nobody knows what stress really is however, or how to avoid stress, remove stress, or how to turn stress into success instead.

This is because of the energy body as the missing X-factor in the equation.

Modern people's energy bodies are in a state of advanced scurvy.

The Scurvy Story

A long time ago, when the first great ships sailed across the oceans of the world, the sailors were beset by many mysterious illnesses.

Their hair and teeth fell out, their bones became weak, their eyesight would deteriorate, their skin would become irritated yet would not heal. The sailors also experienced becoming clumsy and prone to mistakes, falling off the rigging and having more accidents. They couldn't sleep at night and would start to hallucinate and show all the signs of insanity.

The doctors of the time treated each problem separately with all manner of pills, potions and tinctures, but nothing worked – until one doctor finally had the brilliant idea that it was the absence of fresh fruit in their diet.

Just a few drops of lime juice, and all the symptoms went away.

Rather than being all these separate diseases, it was the absence of Vitamin C which was destroying the sailor's minds, bodies and spirits.

The energy bodies of modern humans are living in scurvy conditions.

Nobody knows about the living energy body, no-one takes care of it, and it isn't being fed with the kind of energies the energy body needs to become strong and healthy, to function normally.

There is no pill or potion that can alleviate energy body stress.

We cannot even know what the real energy problems are whilst they are in such poor condition after a lifetime of starvation and malnutrition.

✭ Above all else, we need to start to feed our energy bodies right.

We need to give our energy bodies the energy nutrition they crave – the energy vitamins of powerful, positive energies.

As soon as we do that, the many symptoms of energy body stress start to disappear, and a different person emerges - someone who is stronger, heals faster, who is more powerful, smarter, and most of all, happier.

The Modern Energy Chart

The Modern Energy Chart describes what happens to a person when their energy levels change.

Different energy levels in the energy body create different energy states.

These different energy states create significant changes in a person.

The Energy Chart shows us that any person becomes "a better person" when their energy flow improves.

This improvement is measurable in mental performance, physical performance and in emotional stability.

- **Any human being at all, regardless how old, young, what their gender may be, their previous experiences or current level of health, will improve when energy flow is increased.**

- **Conversely, any human being becomes a worse human being when the energy body is stressed.**

This has very powerful repercussions for a person's self concept.

It finally explains how someone can be sequentially nice and nasty, friendly and antisocial, intelligent and stupid, capable and useless.

⭐ **How well we perform at anything at all is dependent on our energy states.**

To understand this also transforms how we understand other people, and how we deal with them.

To understand that a stressed person is just stressed (rather than "mad, bad and dangerous" or "born bad") allows us to treat them differently, to use very different strategies to help them and bring them back to better states of functioning in mind, body and spirit.

This is of the utmost importance in dealing with children but also with adults, both in private contexts as well as in professional and business relationships.

For personal development and understanding yourself, the Energy Chart is the key to your evolution.

The Energy Chart In Brief

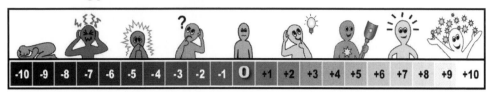

| -10 | -9 | -8 | -7 | -6 | -5 | -4 | -3 | -2 | -1 | 0 | +1 | +2 | +3 | +4 | +5 | +6 | +7 | +8 | +9 | +10 |

We can measure our energy body states and those of other people using the Modern Energy Chart.

This gives us not only important information about the person, but also a direction in which we want to move if we want this person to be more powerful, active, intelligent, capable, physically co-ordinated and emotionally resilient.

We move upward on the Energy Chart when we add more energy to the energy body.

Here are the major energy body states in brief.

The Extremely Low Energy States

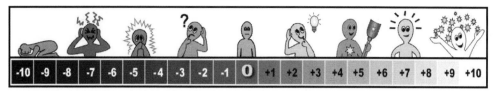

-8 to -10 describes the extremely low energy states that can become life threatening.

It takes many destructive events for energy bodies to become so critically low on energy that they literally collapse in on themselves.

This can be observed in the natural dying process of old people, but also in people following extreme emotional disturbances.

At -8, we find all the symptoms previously associated with severe depression. The person at -8 literally has no energy to help themselves or perform even routine physical functions.

A person at -9 is withdrawn, incapable of making connections with others, incapable of communicating and indeed, struggling to survive at all.

Depending on the circumstances, people will recover slowly as the energy system strives to repair itself, but if the damage is too severe, the person might never fully recover.

-10, the complete extinction of the energy body, leads to physical death shortly after.

The Emergency State At -7

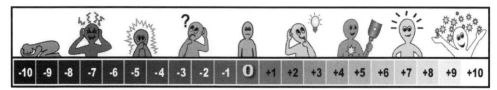

When energy flow has become critical, an emergency response is triggered in the energy system which will throw the last remaining reserves of energy into the system as a survival effort.

The affected person will explode into rage or other uncontrollable emotions, throw themselves around and may attack bystanders randomly.

There is an explosion of energy at -7 which has confused people for a long time.

The emergency generator is not a high energy state, it is a critical survival emergency state that should not be used unless it is really a life or death situation.

The absence of coherent, logical thought, any understanding of moral values or long term consequences of actions in this state makes it particularly dangerous.

Further, there will be an energy collapse after the emergency system has been triggered, into the extreme low energy states, and the health of the energy body may be permanently jeopardized.

Fear

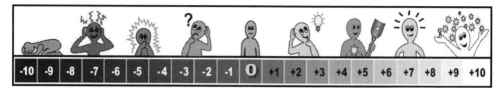

Around -5 we find high stress, anxiety and fear.

This denotes an extremely de-stabilised energy body that is on the verge of flipping into the -7 emergency state, where all conscious control is lost.

The person at -5 and -6 will be incapable of controlling their thoughts or directing their attention. They will be paranoid, fearful, startle easily and find it impossible to concentrate. Their mental abilities and faculties of reasoning are strongly impaired, which can lead to bad decisions.

They will typically experience strong 6th Sense sensations, such as trembling, stomach churning, back aches, headaches etc. and their physical performance will be strongly impaired, making it much more likely that accidents will occur.

When the 6th Sense sensations become overwhelming, individuals might turn to self mutilation to override the psychosomatic pain from their emotions.

Stress

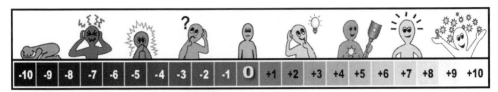

Uncertainty and stress are the keywords for the energy body states between -2 and -4.

This is where the vast majority of the modern population exists on average.

Feeling unsure, unbalanced, not quite right, being easily distracted and not feeling entirely at home in one's own physical body are among the many negative side effects of ongoing low energy states that are deemed to be normal.

Social functioning and communications are strongly impaired, self doubt is a constant feature of this state.

Here we also find pretending to be happier/better/stronger than a person really feels inside and an ongoing rat race of competition as hungry dogs would fight over the a bone.

This is a chronic stress state that relies on applying will power the whole time to create the outward appearance of functionality and happiness.

Under the old systems which did not factor in the states of the energy body, these stress states were deemed to produce maximum effort from the stressed people involved and were mistaken for "good stress."

On the Modern Energy Chart, this is a dangerous energy body stress state and much, MUCH better performance awaits on the other side of Zero.

The Zero Point Of Nothing

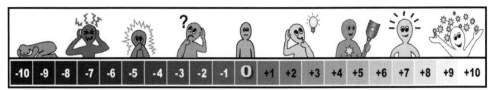

Having ZERO emotions, feeling nothing at all, feeling neither good nor bad, is the deluded and entirely erroneous goal of the old schools of emotional suppression and mismanagement.

ZERO is not a place of balance. When you have zero money in your account, zero food in your fridge and zero friends in your address book, this is what you have – ZERO.

Likewise, we also have ZERO intelligence and ZERO logic in this place that doesn't understand people, doesn't understand emotions, and produces truly inhumane systems that will destroy people who pass through them.

Getting beyond the Zero Point of Nothing, explaining to people that this isn't good enough, it's NOTHING, actually, is the great challenge of Modern Energy.

Yes, it is bad to suffer from negative emotions.

Having no emotions is not the cure.

We need to move forward, into the higher energy states and the realms of positive emotions.

Awakening

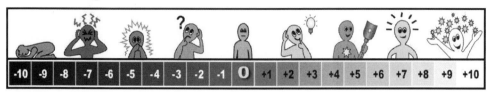

When energy flow finally improves beyond Zero, and the energy body wakes up, so does the person whose energy body this is.

Now, a person may have some ideas about the future, might want to improve something, make positive changes, start a project.

It is important to note that at the low positive ranges, there is enough energy to think, dream and talk about projects, but not enough energy to actually enact them through ongoing, daily, reliable physical labour and high energy activity.

At the social level, a person's social capabilities increase at +3 and they become more attractive to others.

They also become more open-minded, mentally flexible, and able to learn more easily as well as remember better.

As they are now energy positive, they have energy left to give to others.

This is a good first step towards real energy body health which we find not at +3, but at +10 instead.

Action

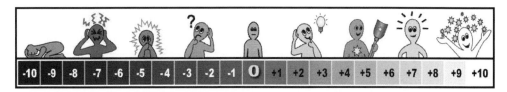

When the energy body gets to +5, we have the energy to take ACTION.

To make anything happen in the real world, we need to put in effort, labour, physical activity, and we have to keep it up on a regular basis.

Many people have good ideas, but to turn these ideas into something real takes a lot of energy, every day.

There will be set backs of course that will drop us down the Energy Chart and we might get angry, stressed, afraid or depressed for a while; but we can bring up our energy average back to above +5 so we can take the action we need to take in the real world in order to succeed.

* A very common problem is seen when people have good ideas, are inspired, get started, but then something bad happens and they run out of steam. Serial failures in everything from learning via relationships and business success come from this cycle, which we can finally both understand, as well as break, with Modern Energy knowledge.

Success

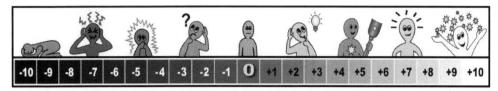

The previous stage, +5, is the set up for success.

Working with lots of energy on something we are excited about, not giving up when there are set backs and fully engaging with our projects will lead to success.

Success is a new level of accomplishment and achievement, and it brings many further rewards.

It raises self esteem, and also allows a person to do energising things, and surround themselves with environments and people that can further raise energy.

A +7 person becomes a natural leader as people will follow those with higher energy states than themselves, and gather a team about them.

From the earthly standpoint, +7 is as good as it gets.

The person has good relationships, is abundant, has many friends and to all intents and purposes, is a role model for success.

Plus Ten

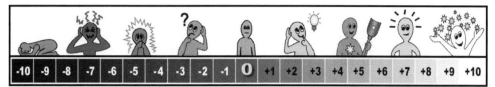

There is a tremendous threshold shift from +7 to +10.

At +10, the energy body fires on all cylinders and this brings a tremendous increase in emotional, physical and mental health.

For as long as human beings have been around, these states were incredibly rare, and people who obtained them by accident or incident were thought to be prophets, saints, geniuses, or otherwise blessed by the stars.

Often, they would bring back a single good idea from these high energy states, where true organic intelligence and real logic are accessible, where cause-and-effect become apparent, where the nature of reality itself becomes revealed to a human being.

Many times, these people would start a revolution, or a religion, or became famous leaders, artists and scientists revered across the ages.

- **The extraordinary truth is that all normal human beings can attain +10 states, and it is actually easy to do so.**

All we have to do is to feed our energy body, and the +10 experiences cease to be a once in a lifetime event, and become the solutions to our individual problems, and those of the human race as well.

Living Life With A Full Battery

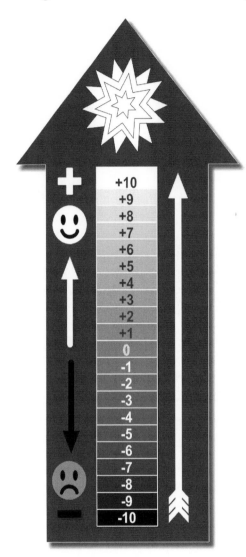

There are all sorts of things modern human beings do which disturb the energy system.

The more stressed the energy system becomes, the worse we feel about ourselves, about other people, about the whole world.

Life becomes hard and painful.

It gets worse as energy flow becomes more and more disrupted.

Low energy flow leads to disturbed emotions, disturbed thinking and makes the body weak as well.

When energy flow is low, we try to live life with a depleted battery.

There is no energy for self healing, never mind self improvement.

We simply don't have the strength to do the work we need to do and we don't have much left to give to others.

We need to learn to quite literally re-charge the batteries of our energy systems - and to do that, we need positive energy that empower the energy system and bring it back to life.

**Positive energy feeds the energy body
and re-charges your batteries of life.**

High Energy Flow

The energy system works best when it is in full flow - above +7 on the Energy Chart.

This is a state similar to when you are in love.

Gravity is lighter, the colours are brighter, you feel strong, young, powerful and happy in every fibre of your being, wide awake, and you are kind to everyone.

To move into these high energy states, we need more POSITIVE energy.

Positive energy lifts our state (of mind, body and spirit!) higher and make us feel glad to be alive.

We become more powerful, but most importantly, more joyful.

This gives us real strength and the energy we need to create the lives we want to lead.

Many Different People: The Aspects Model

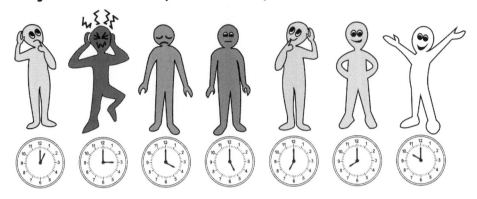

Understanding energy body stress transforms the way we understand ourselves as well as other people.

Every person is many different people - depending on how stressed they are at the time.

To help us understand how this works, we have The Aspects Model in Modern Energy theory.

An aspect is any person who isn't here, right now.

We talk of past aspects and future aspects.

We can be very precise and talk about that aspect of you who was very excited when they were told some good news at 3pm on Wednesday.

This avoids having to squish all these many different people who we really are into a single messy "I."

Instead of thinking/saying, "I am naughty and nice, I am patient and impatient, I am happy and angry, I'm stupid and smart, I'm strong and I'm weak, and none of that makes any sense!"

We say, "I am here. Yesterday around lunch time, my aspect got extremely stressed and did something I wish she had not."

Instead of saying, "Peter is a bully!" we say, "Peter's stressed aspects are bullies. When he's not stressed, his aspects can be really nice."

It takes a little while to get used to referring to one's past aspects and future aspects in that way, but it is well worth it.

For example, a teenage boy was told, "If you leave your shoes there, your aspect tomorrow is going to get all stressed out because he won't find them." For the first time ever, he agreed, picked up his shoes and placed them by his bed – for his morning aspect to find them there.

Relating to aspects, rather than trying to love or forgive "yourself," is much easier and leads to a profound re-unification.

It works with the energy body especially well, as we can direct energy to ourselves in the now, as well to past aspects and future aspects.

The most important lesson of the Aspects Model is this.

- **Everyone has many aspects, and the more stressed the aspects are, the worse they will behave.**

To understand that someone - your child, your partner, your boss, the checkout assistant, the aggressive driver - is simply stressed makes all the difference.

It makes us instantly more compassionate, more patient, and allows us to respond more accurately and positively.

Instead of getting stressed ourselves and falling to into the same stress pit, we can start to think of new and different ways to deal with any situation.

Sometimes it is just a matter of walking away, but often we can help a stressed person become less stressed - and therefore, a better person.

Understanding that everybody can be "good" or "bad" depending where they are on the Energy Chart can also end confusion about "what kind of person you are."

It can help us break out of labels we have been given, and returns us simply to being a normal human being who reacts predictably when stress gets too high.

Most of all, understanding how energy body stress works in people (and in animals, who also have an energy system) gives us a clear route out of trouble and into much better performance all around.

Feed the energy body with Positives.
It's as simple as that. And as profound.

Modern Energy Tapping To Raise Energy

Modern Energy Tapping works by stimulating - tapping on - special energy points to "wake up" the energy body and improve the energy flow in major energy channels.

At the same time, we focus on positive energy – what we know and feel we need more of in our lives.

MET powerfully improves energy flow.

Older forms of tapping were used like psychotherapy to discover traumas and painful memories and to tap for them until a person feels better.

With Modern Energy Tapping, we cut out the middleman of delving into psychotherapy and trauma and instead ask,

"What do you need right now to make you feel better, right away?"

This is much easier and much more practical than trying to get people to psychoanalyse themselves; with Modern Energy Tapping, we get much more gain without any of the pain.

- Modern Energy Tapping is real, modern *energy* work, not psychotherapy in any shape or form

The Modern Energy Tapping protocol is designed to improve energy flow as quickly and profoundly as possible.

Here is how to do Modern Energy Tapping.

Start With The Heart!

Start by placing both hands on the centre of your chest, over the spot where you would point if you pointed to yourself and said, "I, this is me."

This is where your Heart of Energy is located.

By assuming the Heart Position, we are also activating our Hands of Energy, which will do the tapping on the energy body.

The Hands of Energy are also known as "the healing hands."

For practice, assume the Heart Position now, and take three deep breaths, in and out.

How To Do Modern Energy Tapping Right

⭐Practice energy tapping on the back of your hand.

⭐Imagine you are about to touch someone else with your outstretched fingertip.

⭐You love this person very much, and you want to heal them with your touch.

⭐Touch very lightly, as though you were briefly closing an electrical contact.

⭐Pay attention how you can feel that touch.

⭐How far can you feel it moving into your other hand, and up your arm?

⭐Now tap very lightly, short pulses, and keep paying attention how it feels.

⭐Switch hands and tap very lightly on the back of your other hand.

⭐Keep paying attention to the sensations your touch is producing.

⭐Try different rhythms of tapping.

⭐Remember to keep breathing deeply, in and out.

Congratulations!

You have learned to energy tap with the loving touch.

Finding The Right Places To Energy Tap

As we have found out when we were tapping on the back of the hands, the sensations spread out far beyond the place we are energy tapping.

This means that you do not have to worry to get the spot exactly right.

As long as you are energy tapping in the general area, you are doing well.

With a little practice, you start to sense exactly where your tapping energy finger needs to be.

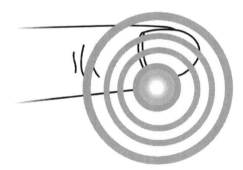

For the finger points, tap on the side of the finger that is facing you, where the nail starts.

Pay attention to the sensations and how far you can track them through your body.

Think ENERGY when you are energy tapping!

The tapping finger is your magic wand.

Now we are ready to start Modern Energy Tapping!

Learning The Energy Tapping Points

Modern Energy Tapping

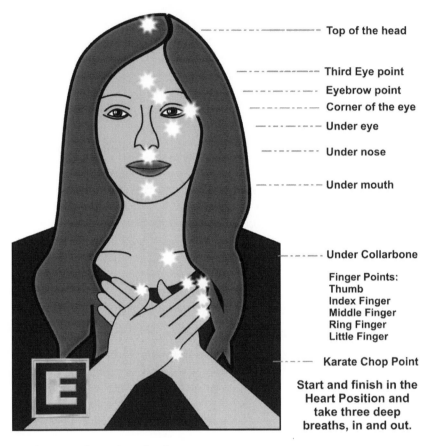

Top of the head

Third Eye point
Eyebrow point
Corner of the eye
Under eye

Under nose

Under mouth

Under Collarbone

Finger Points:
Thumb
Index Finger
Middle Finger
Ring Finger
Little Finger

Karate Chop Point

Start and finish in the Heart Position and take three deep breaths, in and out.

For practise, touch each point in turn.

Take a deep breath, in and out, before moving to the next one.

Pay attention to the sensations you can feel.

Once you have found all the points, go through them a few times quite swiftly, just touching them, to get a feel for the sequence.

Congratulations!

Now you know where the energy tapping points are!

The Modern Energy Tapping Sequence

1. Start with the Heart! Assume the Heart Position with your energy hands on the energy heart, and take three deep breaths in and out.

2. Energy tap the points mindfully. Take a deep breath in and out before moving on to the next point.

3. Finish with the Heart of Energy and take three deep breaths, in and out.

You can practise the MET Sequence at any time to de-stress and re-energize.

You do not have to say anything for practice.

Take your time.

⭐ **Pay attention to your sensations.**

Energy tapping is a beautiful skill, and when you learn how to do this right, all future energy tapping will benefit.

Practise the complete
Modern Energy Tapping Sequence now!

Measuring Your Energy Levels With The SUE Scale

The SUE Scale (Subjective Units of Experience, Hartmann 2009) allows us to measure our energy body state.

The SUE Scale allows us to become consciously aware of how our energy body is doing.

Once we are consciously aware where we are on the SUE Scale, we can choose to feel better.

We can track our progress towards better energy body states on the SUE Scale.

We can use the SUE Scale to have a goal for energy body health and happiness.

On a scale of -10 (dead, or in a coma) and +10 (enlightenment experience), where are you right now?

Slide your finger over the diagram and sense for the right area.

It is alright to find a general region, such as "somewhere between -2 and +2" to get started.

Do this now and find out where you are right now on the SUE Scale.

What is your SUE number?

Raising ENERGY!

For our first Positive, we are going to energy tap for ENERGY.

Having more ENERGY to live, love, work and play is a wonderful gift.

Take a moment to think about what you could do if you had a lot more ENERGY.

Think about a future self, a future aspect who has lots of energy.

Make sure you are on board with really wanting more ENERGY in YOUR life.

 This is important! If you energy tap for something that you don't care about, nothing much will happen. The more you want the positive energy, the better this will work.

- **Now, assume the Heart Position.**
- **Take three deep breaths in and out.**
- **Say out aloud, "I want more ENERGY!"**
- **Energy tap all the points. On each one say out aloud, "ENERGY!"**
- **Pay attention to any physical 6th Sense sensations this produces.**
- **Energy tap all the way through the points.**
- **End in the Heart Position and take three deep breaths.**

Check the SUE Scale.

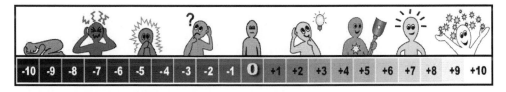

| -10 | -9 | -8 | -7 | -6 | -5 | -4 | -3 | -2 | -1 | 0 | +1 | +2 | +3 | +4 | +5 | +6 | +7 | +8 | +9 | +10 |

What is your SUE number now?

Feeling Better

What was your first SUE number, and what was your SUE number after the Modern Energy Tapping sequence?

Even if you only experienced a small shift of a single point …

CONGRATULATIONS!

You have done something amazing.

You have changed your energy state, simply by Modern Energy Tapping, in a very short period of time.

With practice and experience, this gets better and better.

> ⭐ **Your shifts will become stronger.**
>
> ⭐ **Your energy experiences will become more powerful.**

You have taken the first step towards emotional mastery.

From now on, Modern Energy Tapping will become more and more exciting.

**The power of
all the Positives in the Universe
are at <u>YOUR</u> fingertips.**

Tips On Modern Energy Tapping

- Choose Positives that have a strong, emotional meaning for you.

- The more you want, need and crave THAT energy, the better Modern Energy Tapping will work for you.

- Talk out aloud, let your voice be heard, really evoke the Positive.

- You don't have to close your eyes or concentrate too hard. Just focus on the Positive, and let the tapping do the magic.

- Remember: It is your energy hands tapping on your energy body doing the work in MET.

- Tapping "harder" isn't going to help. Instead, pay attention to the feeling of the contact between your fingertips and your body; tapping should feel pleasant and relaxing to you. Experiment with how to energy tap so it feels GREAT to you!

- Tap lightly and rhythmically, using your index finger.

- Breathe deeply while you tap.

- Always take time for one deep breath in and out between points.

- Keep relaxed as you tap. Loosen your shoulders, relax your face, your neck and your arms, your wrist, hand and fingers as this helps with energy flow.

- Energy tapping works much better when you're standing up.

- Move your body to keep it loose and relaxed.

- Move your body in response to the energy sensations to help the energy flow increase faster.

- Really think about the Positive you are tapping for, think about what it means to you, how much you want it.

- Allow yourself to be emotional - emotions are energy and the more energy you can put in, the more energy you will get out.

- Practice lots, with lots of different Positives.

- All Positives are good for you!

- You cannot choose the wrong Positive!

Energy Tapping Positives

An energy Positive is any kind of energy you want more of in your life.

Mind, body and spirit are supposed to work together, all three doing the same thing at the same time.

When we energy tap for Positives,

- We focus the mind by speaking the word/s out aloud,

- We engage the body by touching physically,

- We are stimulating the energy body.

The more attractive the positive energy is to you, the easier it is to get good results.

Overleaf is a list of Positives you can choose from to get you started.

- **Choose something you really want in your life.**

Put both hands on your chest in the Heart Position, take three deep breaths and say the name of the Positive out aloud.

⭐ *A tip: Think of saying the word like you would call someone by name to come to you. "Energy! Over here! Come to me!"*

Then lightly tap all of the special energy points, starting from the top of the head.

On each point, call out the name of the Positive loudly and clearly as you tap.

Take a deep breath in and out, then move on to the next point.

Finish in the Heart Position and take three deep breaths.

Choose a first Positive of your own now.

A First List Of Energy Positives

Love	Youth	Steel	Home
Wisdom	Wealth	Magic	Lightning
Logic	Play	Creativity	Luck
Wonder	Power	Sanctuary	Strength
Money	Fame	Stillness	Sunshine
Mystery	Pride	Tranquillity	Angel
Confidence	Serenity	Union	Freedom
Excitement	Blessings	Rhythm	Harmony
Hope	Vision	Diversity	Beauty
Health	Evolution	Space	Success
Purpose	Satisfaction	Surprise	Grace
Clarity	Resonance	Sex	Time
Lifting	Transformation	Fun	Lightness
Kindness	Tenderness	Inspiration	Treasures
Abundance	Immortality	Joy	Truth
Happiness	Stability	Fortune	Vitality
Dance	Focus	Gold	Gratitude
Faith	Certainty	Wisdom	Connection
Laughter	Dominion	Effortless	Soul
Miracle	Energy	Respect	Luck
Brilliance	Belonging	Expansion	Trust

Which Positive would make you feel better, right away?

- Don't choose with your head, choose with your heart.
- Find a Positive that makes you feel emotional.
- Don't worry about choosing the "right" Positive.
- The Positives won't go away.

    Just choose the Positive you want to have MORE of, **right now.**

MORE Energy ...

A first Modern Energy Tapping sequence will raise our energy levels.

You can tell when energy flow becomes higher when ...

- You start to feel tingling in your body

- You feel lighter, happier, stronger

- You start to relax, move more freely

- You start to breathe more freely and more deeply

- You smile or laugh.

This is an improvement, but we can go much further than that!

We can energy tap another sequence for the same Positive to increase energy flow further.

Use the same Positive for the next sequence and simply add MORE.

So this time, we do the MET sequence from the Heart Position through to the Heart Position at the end and as we tap, we say loudly and strongly:

I want MORE ..!

Allow yourself to really, really want more (...) in your life, right now.

This creates a powerful energy movement you can really FEEL in your body - and it feels GOOD!

We were born to feel good.

We are designed to FEEL GOOD!

Even MORE Energy ...

We are not taking anything away from anyone else, because it's only energy so don't be shy!

Do another sequence of Modern Energy Tapping straight after and allow yourself to invite:

EVEN MORE ..!!!

And one more sequence - it only takes about two minutes for each one! and we can tap for ...

ALL THE ... IN THE UNIVERSE!!!

Fantastic!

When the energy starts to flow through your body, MOVE!

Get up, walk around while you energy tap. Dance!

Feel your energy body come to life – and feel what that does to your physical body, and to your mind.

Important Points About Modern Energy Tapping

1. Allow Yourself To Really WANT Positive Energy!

When you pick a Positive, take a moment to allow yourself to really, REALLY want it.

The more "hungry" you can allow yourself to be, the more of a tidal draw you create in your energy system, and the more energy can flow into you as a direct result.

It is important to understand that you don't need to know how more (luck, joy, sex, wealth, power, respect etc. etc.) is going to come into your life as a result of what you are doing here.

It also doesn't matter at all if you think you deserve it or not, and you don't even have to know exactly what that "means" - all you have to do from your end is to WANT IT.

We want these things which money can't buy; they are positive energies which create emotions and sensations we can feel, and which make us feel good.

It is right and natural to fill the wants and needs of your particular energy body, just as it is right and natural to drink water when you are thirsty, or eat something when you are hungry.

⭐ **The more we feed our energy bodies with the energies they have hungered for all their lives, the better we feel.**

Nature rewards us for doing the right thing! We all have been taught that it is bad to want things, that we should make due or learn to go without. When we work with Modern Energy Tapping, we need to let go of that and allow ourselves to want these Positives with the same intensity a small child would have who wants a particular toy.

This is an important part of working with Modern Energy Tapping and a wonderful side effect - we become much clearer on what we want in our lives, and that makes it much easier to get many other things too, including material changes we might have sought but which always seemed so out of reach.

2. It's Only Real If You Can Feel It's Real!

Working with Modern Energy Tapping is NOT "positive thinking" or "tapping in affirmations."

Positive thinking and saying things that aren't true doesn't work when your energy system is stressed and miserable. In fact, it can make us feel even worse.

Energy Tapping on a Positive is a very different experience.

As we tap and say, "I want ENERGY!" we are simply speaking the truth; and as energy begins to flow more freely, we can really feel the effects in our physical bodies.

This is our real 6th Sense, the sense that informs us about energy.

Pay attention to:

- **Tingling sensations in your body** - those are often the first indications that energy flow is starting up.

- **Shivers and other sensations that make you want to move** (your neck, your shoulders, your feet, your back) - it's important to stay loose and go with those sensations, that helps energy flow much better.

- **Yawning, tearing of the eyes, waves of strange sensations** - that happens when energy blockages start to dissolve and are all natural reactions to improving the energy flow.

- **Floaty feelings, feeling very relaxed, sleepy** - that's what happens around the 0 point on the SUE scale, and it's a sign you are coming up from a stressed state towards better energy flow. It's very important to keep on energy tapping, you're on the right path!

It's the sensations, the feelings in your body, which are the most important. That's what is telling you something is changing.

This is your true 6th Sense. It is the direct body sensations that tell us, "Yes, you really have an energy body, and yes, something amazing is happening!"

If you don't feel anything much on your first sequence, don't despair.

Many people, and especially men, have been trained to ignore their 6th Sense and "not to feel any emotions."

It takes a while to re-direct your attention to your body sensations.

Energy awareness and being able to improve your energy flow gets better and stronger with practise, so choose another Positive and do some more Modern Energy Tapping!

Choose another Positive for practice now and find out how good it feels!

Love	Youth	Steel	Home
Wisdom	Wealth	Magic	Lightning
Logic	Play	Creativity	Luck
Wonder	Power	Sanctuary	Strength
Money	Fame	Stillness	Sunshine
Mystery	Pride	Tranquillity	Angel
Confidence	Serenity	Union	Freedom
Excitement	Blessings	Rhythm	Harmony
Hope	Vision	Diversity	Beauty
Health	Evolution	Space	Success
Purpose	Satisfaction	Surprise	Grace
Clarity	Resonance	Sex	Time
Lifting	Transformation	Fun	Lightness
Kindness	Tenderness	Inspiration	Treasures
Abundance	Immortality	Joy	Truth
Happiness	Stability	Fortune	Vitality
Dance	Focus	Gold	Gratitude
Faith	Certainty	Wisdom	Connection
Laughter	Dominion	Effortless	Soul
Miracle	Energy	Respect	Luck
Brilliance	Belonging	Expansion	Trust

Energy is FREE!

3. Loosen Up For Maximum Energy Flow

This is important:

The more you can loosen up your physical body, the faster your energy flow will increase and the better you will feel.

Don't screw up your eyes in furious concentration; instead, breathe deeply, relax your shoulders, and MOVE with the 6th Sense sensations that the energy tapping produces in your body.

Energy Tapping whilst standing up helps a lot.

Opening a window for some fresh air is a good idea.

Shaking out your hands and feet in between rounds, rotating your neck and loosening up your ankles, knees, hips and spine really helps with energy flow too.

When the energy flow becomes fast and high, it is natural to be dancing around the room - that's a good sign you're getting this right!

4. It's Really OK To Feel Good!

- **Whoever you are and whatever you do, it really is OK for you to feel good.**

The more often you can feel on top of the world, the more stress you are releasing at the same time, and the better your life is going to start to work for you, in every department.

Being happy doesn't make you silly, or irresponsible, or weak - just the opposite.

- **In order to be the best person we can possibly be, we need to feel happy and strong inside as often as possible.**

We need to fill our lives with GOOD experiences, good feelings and then we have something to give to others as well.

So please say **YES!!!** to joy, and luck, and love and all the many other Positives that money can't buy - but we can experience in our own living bodies, thanks to Modern Energy Tapping.

The American Policeman

I was talking to an American policeman, and he was 100% convinced that not having any emotions at all was the only way he could do his job.

I was astonished by that notion – until I understood that when he used the term "emotion," he was only thinking of negative emotions.

Getting angry, getting sad, getting stressed, getting distressed.

I said to him, "But wouldn't it really help in your job if you were on top form, full of energy, really aware of everything, clear and powerful?"

He looked at me in astonishment, blinked many times, and said, "Well ... I hadn't thought of it like that ..."

Being on the positive side of the Energy Chart is a GOOD THING!

Discovering Modern Energy Tapping - In Brief

- We have energy bodies which have been neglected.

- The energy body is connected to the physical body through the 6th Sense – physical sensations that have no physical origin.

- When we are energy rich, we experience powerful positive emotions.

- When the energy body becomes stressed, energy poor, we experience negative emotions.

- Stressed energy bodies lead to negative emotions, disturbed thought, bad behaviour and will eventually also affect health.

- To reverse energy body stress, we need positive energies which feed the energy system and make it stronger.

- We can know what kinds of positive energies we need because we can feel what we need.

- Money can't buy the feelings of joy, respect, luck and all the other positive energies - but we HUNGER for them.

- Modern Energy Tapping is a quick and easy way to improve energy flow and start to feel much, much better – fast and reliably.

- The more often we can feel better, the more we reduce overall energy body stress and the more effortless and successful life becomes.

- If you can allow yourself a positive energy experience as often as you brush your teeth, your life will transform within the year - guaranteed.

- With practice, evoking and experiencing the power of the Positives gets faster, better, and easier.

So don't delay -
Start energy tapping YOUR Positives today!

Part 2 - From Stress To Success

"Understand negative emotions and negative thoughts as energy body stress, and your entire life will change for the better."

Silvia Hartmann

Understanding Energy Body Stress

The biggest breakthrough in Modern Energy has been the understanding of the effects of energy body stress.

We have discovered that not only negative emotions, but also ...

- negative self concepts

- lack of self belief

- lack of confidence

- fear and anxiety

- negative thinking

- inability to have good relationships

- and performance failures

... are all just "signs of stress" and nothing more.

> ⭐ **As soon as energy flow improves and a person moves up the Energy Chart, all manner of negative emotions, thoughts and behaviours simply disappear without a trace.**

Conversely, every normal person starts to feel, think and do all sorts of negative things when they are under stress.

This explains so much, including why we sometimes think we're great and we can make it, and at other times think we are idiots and doomed to failure.

When you understand this, negative thoughts and emotions become nothing more than a sign that you are stressed, and you need to add some positive energy to your energy body.

When the stress recedes, so do the negative thoughts, beliefs and feelings, and instead, you "come back to your senses."

Here is a typical example of how this works.

This is a normal young woman and her thoughts about her looks, depending on her energy levels at the time.

One Person, 21 Different "Beliefs"

-10	
-9	I should never have been born. I wish I was dead.
-8	The world would be better off without me.
-7	I am a hideous monstrosity.
-6	I am horribly ugly
-5	I am so ugly
-4	Everything about me is wrong.
-3	My nose is too big, my breasts too small, my bottom is huge.
-2	I don't like the way I look.
-1	Not looking my best today.
0	It will have to do …
1	I guess I look OKish …
2	Not too bad today …
3	I look alright
4	My hair looks nice today
5	I quite like the way I look
6	I am good looking
7	I love the way I look
8	I am beautiful
9	I am amazing!
10	I am a beloved child of the Universe.

The big mistake in the past was to think that there was some kind of "reason" or "root cause" for this lady to feel so bad about herself sometimes.

It was erroneously believed that by going back into the past and dealing with one single childhood trauma (if the right one could be found!) would solve the problem forever.

We have learned that the kind of "negative thinking" and the "negative emotions" this lady is expressing on the negative side of the Energy Chart is just energy body stress manifesting itself.

Stress this lady, and she will predictably feel worse and worse about herself, the lower her energy levels become.

Increase the energy flow, make this lady happy and she will immediately not just change her mood, but also *change her mind.*

Learn To Recognise Your Own Stress

- **<u>Everyone</u> starts to think negative thoughts and will have negative feelings when they get stressed.**

It is normal, completely human and means nothing "about you as a person" other than that you have become stressed.

Bringing positive energy into the energy body is the remedy for chronic energy body stress.

When does it happen in your life that you regularly or often experience the kind of stress that leads to "stress thinking" and negative emotions?

Over the next week, simply pay attention to where and when it happens.

As soon as you realise that your energy has become too low, you are stressed and thinking all sorts of "nonsense thoughts" - the kind of thoughts you would never think if you were feeling powerful and happy! - STOP and pick a Positive to treat yourself.

Understand negative emotions and negative thoughts as energy body stress, and your entire life will change for the better.

Establishing Quick Stress Stoppers – The PPPs

Once you have energy tapped for a particular Positive, you can use it again in a moment of crisis and it will work more quickly for you. The experience also becomes more powerful, every time you use that Positive.

A Positive that really works for you therefore becomes a quick stress stopper, something you can remember in a moment of crisis and even just thinking about it, or thinking about energy tapping for it, can already stabilise you.

- **We call these special Positives our Personal Power Positives or PPPS.**

The lady in our example choose BEAUTY as her Personal Power Positive. After the first time she energy tapped for it, five sequences in all to get all the way to a +10 and feeling delighted, she used looking in the mirror as her stress indicator.

If she liked what she saw, she knew her energy levels were good; if she did not, she knew she was stressed. She would tap just one sequence of BEAUTY to bring her energy system back online, and all was well with the world.

After a week she reported that she just had to think BEAUTY without even having to energy tap for it any longer, and about a month later she realised that she didn't even have to do that any longer. Only on very rare occasions was her stress high enough to make her dislike her own mirror image now.

This is the progression of what happens with Modern Energy Tapping.

The most important part is not just that this lady is steady in her beauty now, her self concept has improved radically, or that she no longer self mutilates in front of the mirror.

The most important thing is that she has learned that negative thoughts and emotions are ONLY STRESS - and what to do to get out of stress as quickly as possible.

- **Learn to recognise when you are stressed - then take POSITIVE action to make yourself feel better.**

My Own Personal Power Positives

What Positive would really help you when you get stressed?

Make a list of PPPs for the situations where you become stressed.

Here is an example:

Stress Problem:	Personal Power Positive:
Work stress	CONNECTION
Relationships stress	FAITH
Health stress	VITALITY
Sex stress	LIGHTNING
Societal stress	RESPECT
Global stress	TRANSFORMATION
Spiritual stress	GRACE
General stress	SUNSHINE

Now create your own Personal Power Positives:

What kind of stress?	The Positive Energy Solution:

Keep this list to hand and practice Modern Energy Tapping on each one of your chosen Personal Power Positives.

Really go for a +10 energy experience every time.

Find out not just how much better it makes you feel but also how it changes the way you think.

Personal Power Positives are very useful!

Allow Yourself To Be GREEDY!

Greed is held to be a terribly bad thing; but it really is only something that happens when a person is more than just hungry for something – they are desperate, starving.

A starving man isn't being greedy.

Learn to think "desperately hungry" instead of "greedy."

Energy is free; it is everywhere and there is more than enough to go around.

- **The sun shines on every one of 8 billion people, and none of us have to share its light - each one gets their own rays, every time!**

It is the same with energy. You are not taking any energy away from someone else. There are literally Oceans of Energy from which we can take in our fill.

We need to allow ourselves to notice what each one of us is "greedy" for - desperately hungry.

Be honest with yourself - what is it that you really want and need and CRAVE in your life above all else?

This is only energy - all you have to do is want it, say it, FEEL IT and allow that energy in.

This will feed your energy body, lift your mood and make your body happier - it's a good thing all around, a healthy thing to be doing.

Your Happiness Matters!

We have been endlessly exhorted all our lives long to put the happiness of others before our own happiness.

This is worse than trying to put the cart before the horse.

On an air plane, mothers with children are advised to put the oxygen masks on themselves first. The reason is that if the mother tries to put the mask on the child first, she will probably faint before this has been accomplished, and then both mother *and* child will die.

If we try to sacrifice ourselves and make ourselves miserable in the service of others, we are in the same position. Our so called service will produce no happiness in others either, and nobody wins.

- **In order to make other people happy, you need energy.**

You need to have something to give in order to give it.

This is why your happiness matters so much.

It is absolutely of the essence to take care of your own energy body so that it becomes healthy, stress free and ready to give all the gifts of support, love, compassion, intelligence and unique contribution you have to give.

You are the gift that only you would have to give.

Your happiness matters.

The Energy Billionaire

Adding the worlds of energy to the physical world changes everything.

In the energy world, there are no limitations at all.

Our energy body can recover and thrive in the Oceans of Energy, and as a totality, we can have all the emotions and experiences we could ever want.

Energy Is Free!

Advertising agencies know they're not selling a car, a wristwatch or a house, they're really selling an energy experience - feelings, emotions, states.

The people who understand this amass fantastic fortunes and reap the rewards of having absolutely everything in physical reality that money can buy.

This is the tiny minority. It's not how the other half lives. Less than 0.0001% of the world's population owns 99% of all material resources. The vast majority of people live in endless poverty conditions, always wanting and dreaming of things they cannot have, they can't afford, will never have …

This creates stress, it creates sadness, it creates anger, bitterness, envy, and every one of the negative emotions that we now know are nothing but low energy states.

Here is the good news.

You no longer have to be rich in order to experience all manner of rich experiences!

- **We can use the material things we crave and convert them into energy at any time, simply and easily.**

That makes us then less desperate, less greedy, less hungry - and thereby many times more likely to actually get what we want in the physical world as well.

The Energy Of Total Abundance

Convert whatever your heart desires, or your stomach, or any other part of your (energy) body into energy simply by adding the word "energy" at the end.

What would you love to experience today ...?

I want!!!

- **Diamond Necklace ENERGY**

- **Great Country Mansion ENERGY**

- **Penthouse ENERGY**

- **Rolex Watch ENERGY**

- **Private Jet ENERGY**

- **Mountains Of Money ENERGY**

- **Lamborghini ENERGY**

- **Luxury Yacht ENERGY**

- **Red Carpet ENERGY**

- **My Own Tropical Island ENERGY**

- **Lottery Win ENERGY ...**

What have you always, always wanted really badly but "you knew you would never be able to afford it"?

Name it, then put the word ENERGY behind it and start a first sequence of Modern Energy Tapping NOW!

If you can feel, walk and talk and act like a million dollars, that's the start to getting whatever you want out of life - and that's a fact.

With the painful hunger for material objects out of the way, we can have a look at other types of Positives to make our energy bodies sparkle!

Healing Nature Energy

Nature energies are the perfect power to revitalise us.

Indeed, the disconnection from nature, being inside too much, living in heated and air conditioned boxes has a lot to do with malnutrition of the energy body.

With Modern Energy Tapping, we can draw in wonderfully nourishing nature energy at any time, anywhere, and feel amazingly recharged and refreshed.

Sunshine	Moonlight	Starlight
Ocean Waves	White Sands	Summer Beach
Beach Party	Blue Sky	Autumn Gold
Spring Fresh	Summer Sun	Winter White
Cathedral Forests	Blue Lagoon	Majestic Mountains
Golden Desert	Valley Green	Sparkling Brook
Mountain Lake	Sunlit Sea	Stately River
Tropical Beach	Winter Woods	Ocean Breeze
Alpine Meadow	Green Grass	Fairy Well
Waterfall	Evening Breeze	Summer Rain
Rain Storm	Lightning	White Clouds
Jungle	Rose Garden	Deep Woods
Snowy Mountains	Sunrise	Dawn
Dusk	Ocean Waves	Shooting Star

Try the energizing power of nature energy as an energy Positive now!

Holiday Energy Positives

Make your own list nature energy Positives and notice how you are drawn to different kinds of nature energies at different times in your life.

- **Your energy body can go on holiday at any time it needs one!**

What places on Earth (or beyond!) are you personally drawn to most strongly?

Where have you always yearned to visit for a holiday?

You can also use memories of favourite holiday moments to raise that holiday feeling.

Where were your favourite places that really made you feel amazing, alive, happy?

Here are a few examples:

- **Niagara ENERGY**

- **Swiss Mountains ENERGY**

- **Monte Carlo ENERGY**

- **Great Lakes ENERGY**

- **New York ENERGY**

- **Great Pyramids ENERGY**

- **Pacific Shore ENERGY**

- **Island Paradise ENERGY**

- **North Pole ENERGY**

- **Himalayas ENERGY**

Now make a list of your own!

It's a great idea to develop your own favourite energy holiday Positives. You will find with a little practice that just thinking towards these begins to lift your mood and your mind noticeably.

Add some Modern Energy Tapping, and you can buzz with real holiday energy all year round!

Animal Power Positives

For as long as people have been around, animal energy has been used to empower us.

- **Animal power is pure, clean and .. very powerful!**

Perhaps you already have a special power animal in your life. Add Modern Energy Tapping and find out what happens when you really run this energy, all the way to a +10.

You can also pick an animal you are drawn to right now, or one that jumps out at you from this list.

Take a moment and give yourself the gift of animal energy now!

Eagle	Lion	Tiger
Leopard	Cheetah	Wolf
Raven	Elephant	Horse
Dog	Cobra	Monkey
Spider	Lizard	Bull
Deer	Antelope	Frog
Crocodile	Dolphin	Camel
Giraffe	Zebra	Buzzard
Heron	Starling	Whale
Killer Whale	Pig	Salmon
Beaver	Weasel	Rat
Cat	Panther	Reindeer
Meerkat	Shark	Owl
Swallow	Boa	Hawk

Oceans Of Energy

Once you start to understand what the Positives are and what they feel like, you can find the Positives absolutely everywhere. You begin to realise that we really do live amongst the "Oceans of Energy" - free energy everywhere, all the time, and for life.

All we have to do is to let it in.

Here are further examples of Positives that can be used to feed your energy body, make stress disappear and strengthen you at any time.

Colour Energy Positives

Ask yourself, which colour would really lift my mood, right now?

You can choose from this list or think of your own special colour.

You can also look around in your environment to find a colour that will be perfect energy nutrition for your energy body right now.

Red	Yellow	Green
Black	Pink	Blue
Purple	Turquoise	Orange
White	Silver	Grey
Royal Blue	Navy Blue	Sea Blue
Aquamarine	Rose	Brown
Cerulean	Lime Green	Apricot
Salmon Pink	Amber	Azure
Lavender	Lemon Yellow	Crimson
Scarlet	Magenta	Cyan
Golden Yellow	Fuchsia	Moss Green
Sky Blue	Vermilion	Golden Brown
Wine Red	Umber	Tangerine
Maroon	Coral Pink	Ultraviolet

Try this and energy tap for, "I want more (turquoise) ENERGY!"

Crystal Energy Positives

Ask yourself, which crystal energy would really lift my mood, right now?

Crystals and minerals are full of powerful nature energy. They have clarity and logic in their very structures and each one is different.

Diamond	Sapphire	Ruby
Emerald	Lapis Lazuli	Jet
Amethyst	Clear Quartz	White Quartz
Rose Quartz	Turquoise	Opal
Citrine	Garnet	Peridot
Haematite	Agate	Aquamarine
Topaz	Alexandrite	Seraphenite
Adventurine	Beryl	Carnelian
Labradorite	Malachite	Tanzanite
Tiger Eye	Sunstone	Magnetite
Onyx	Fluorite	Obsidian

Energy tap for, "I want more (diamond) ENERGY!"

Plant Energy Positives

The power of green is deeply healing, supportive and nourishing at the deepest levels of our energy bodies.

Ask yourself, which plant energy would really lift my mood, right now?

Fir	Rose	Oak
Birch	Lemon	Lavender
Giant Redwood	Willow	Orchid
Cherry	Grass	Lily
Elm	Wintergreen	Lotus
Violet	Fern	Palm Tree
Mangrove	Pine	Bamboo
Cactus	Aloe Vera	Ivy
Parsley	Bluebell	Maple
Moss	Lichen	Mushroom
Apple Tree	Wheat	Wild Flower
Hollyhock	Garlic	Chestnut
Marigold	Foxglove	Eucalyptus
Sage	Dandelion	Poppy

It is interesting to note that we are only dealing with ENERGY here, which is different from the physical properties of the plants. In this way, we can make use of the plant energy even if we do not like the look, taste or smell of the physical plant.

Food Energy Positives

Food energy Positives are very interesting to play around with. For many people, the physical sensations produced through the 6th Sense by the energy body can be mis-interpreted as signals of physical hunger.

This leads to the physical body being fed, but the energy body remains starving and keeps putting out hunger signals.

Experimenting with Positives relating to food can be extremely interesting, especially when it comes to "cravings."

Try feeding the energy body first with a sequence or two of Modern Energy Tapping, for example, "I want some CAKE ENERGY!" If the craving goes away and is fully satisfied, you can know this was an energy body craving. If it does not, it might be time to give the physical body some physical cake! :-)

Cake	Steak	Ice Cream
Cheese	Chips	Curry
Sunday Roast	Seafood	Jelly
Sandwich	Sushi	Barbecue
Hot Soup	Burger	Spaghetti
Pie	Pizza	Pot Roast
Salad	Sweets	Sausage
Fresh Fruit	Cookie	Chocolate
Macaroni	Cup Cake	Custard
Fried Chicken	Bacon	Waffles

Bon Appetit!

People Energy Positives

When we are lonely or feel disconnected from other people, our energy bodies are very stressed. We are a social species and are supposed to make energy connections between one another. Today's world makes this ever more difficult – and our energy bodies are paying the price.

There are many ways to use the power of the Positives with energy relationships to other people.

If you had more of this, would your life become easier? Happier?

⚝ **Friendship ENERGY**

⚝ **Community ENERGY**

⚝ **Family ENERGY**

⚝ **Partner ENERGY**

⚝ **Child ENERGY**

⚝ **Parental ENERGY**

⚝ **Peer ENERGY**

⚝ **Ancestral ENERGY**

⚝ **PEOPLE ENERGY**

It is much better for the energy body, who is aching for this connection with other people, to energy tap than to sit in the dark and cry.

At the energy levels, we are much more connected than we think we are.

When there is better energy flow at the energy levels, there is a much better chance that relationships in physical reality start to work better as well.

Learning to be more empowered by positive people energy is extremely healing for the energy body, and there are many other ways in which to restore and activate our natural people connections.

Hero Energy Positives

Every person has their own heroes – people who have inspired them, helped them, loved them or were loved by them.

This is a very special kind of energy we can evoke when we do Modern Energy Tapping. This can give us inspiration, strength and much love and joy, quickly, simply and directly.

Who are your heroes?

Superhero Energy - Young aspects may have wanted to be like SuperMan. This is an entirely fictional character but it has a unique "SuperMan ENERGY!" which works wonderfully well in Modern Energy Tapping.

You can use this for your own aspects and it is quite delightful.

You can also use this with children to great effect. Try it for yourself!

Family Hero Energy - Hopefully, every child had at least one person in their family to whom they could look up and who was loved by them.

Evoking that person's energy directly by name is extremely powerful and supportive.

For example, energy tapping for "Grandma Mary ENERGY" is a wonderful experience.

Teacher Hero Energy - Which teacher inspired your aspects? Which teachers do you still remember fondly today? They may have been physical teachers, or perhaps an aspect read a book or watched a video. Re-igniting that energy connection to a hero teacher can do much for us, especially when we feel in need of support.

Human Hero Energy - We are inspired by many different kinds of people. Some are in our families, some we have met, some we have never met at all, some entirely fictional.

Whoever has inspired your aspects in the past, or who inspires you still today is a powerful Positive for you.

Energy tap their name plus ENERGY.

It is a wonderful experience.

We really do live in the Oceans of Energy.

In this section, we have met many, many powerful Positives just to get us started.

★ **Total Abundance Energy Positives**

★ **Healing Nature Energy Positives**

★ **Holiday Energy Positives**

★ **Animal Power Positives**

★ **Colour Energy Positives**

★ **Crystal Energy Positives**

★ **Plant Energy Positives**

★ **Food Energy Positives**

★ **People Energy Positives**

★ **Hero Energy Positives**

These are just some examples of wonderful, energy packed occurrences on this world of ours that we can use to really lift our spirit in the true sense of the word, at any time, anywhere.

Learn to find your own favourite Positives - start looking out for new Positives!

I've Got THAT Feeling ...

Sometimes, we can't even put into words what we want or feel exactly.

This doesn't mean that we can't energy tap for it.

There are definitely sensations and feelings beyond words, and if you got one of those, or you need on of those, simply use, "THAT feeling!" because you know exactly what you mean by that.

We can use positive feelings we remember from the past as a starting point to feel good now and bring us even better energy for the now, and for the future.

For example ...

Remember a time when you felt absolutely wonderful. Take a moment to really remember when that was, how that happened, what the weather was, where you were at the time. Now, remember the feeling and start a sequence of Modern Energy Tapping, tapping simply for ...

"THAT feeling!"

You can use the same pattern for THAT feeling and really go for it, tapping the next sequence for, "I want even more of THAT feeling!" and the following rounds for "I want all THAT feeling in the universe!" to get your energy flow really high.

This is a very useful thing that stops us from trying to re-live the glories of the past (that's doomed to failure!) or mistakenly thinking that all the good experiences are in the past now, especially as we get older.

Emotional energy experiences do not need to be linked to physical events at all, and once we learn how to feel good when we want to feel good (rather than sitting around and waiting and hoping it will happen mysteriously somehow) it is in our hands just how much fun we are going to have on every given day.

As far as we know, human beings are the only creatures on Earth ever to have been able to do that, so let us celebrate this amazing gift and use it to its fullest potential!

Bigger & Better Visions, Goals & Dreams

"People without dreams are angels with broken wings."
Silvia Hartmann

Visions, goals and dreams are positive energy constructs we put out into the future and which inspire us.

- **"To inspire" means to put extra energy into us so that we come to life, become stronger, healthier and happier.**

To have a vision, goal or dream in your life is essential and priceless.

The further down the stress chart you go and the less energy you have, the further away visions, goals and dreams become until they disappear behind the stress horizon altogether.

That's a terrible thing when that happens; it is potentially soul destroying.

The more energy flow there is, the stronger and more powerfully energizing visions, goals and dreams become. It's just like a sun rise in many ways.

Successful people always talk about their goals inspire them and how these goals give them the strength to work harder, to try harder, to "keep their eye on the ball," not be distracted by things that don't matter, and how to find that all important inspiration even in the darkest hours.

So now, let's talk about your visions, goals and dreams.

It doesn't matter what they are, and once again, please allow yourself to be honest.

Your visions don't have to be for the good of the world, nor do your goals have to sound "nice" to the kind of audience you would find at a Miss Universe competition.

You know what's in your heart, what you want out of life, what is important to achieve in this lifetime.

Now, this is very important.

- We are working with the **energy** of visions, goals and dreams.

It doesn't matter if you are too old now to ever win the 100m sprint at the Olympic games in the Hard.

"Gold Medal ENERGY" is something you can have at any time in your life.

Likewise, it doesn't matter if you have never succeeded at anything, if you have a string of business failures behind you or if you have no idea how to get closer to manifesting your vision, your goal or your dream.

Think about your vision, goal or dream for a moment.

Give it a name or a title, so we can speak it out aloud.

For example, a person might have the goal of becoming a hugely successful Modern Energy trainer and teaching huge, grateful and delighted audiences all over the world about how to be happier. And these audiences will go out into their worlds and help their fellow human beings to be happier. And this spreads out in ripples, until all of humanity is more energized and many wonderful changes happen …

This person decided to call their vision "The Happiness Catalyst" and so they energy tapped for "Happiness Catalyst Energy!"

They also wrote this particular Positive on a piece of card and affixed it to their notice board, to use as a Personal Power Positive at any time they started to feel stressed, unsure, or disconnected from their work and their vision.

This is an extremely powerful way to keep on track with your visions and goals, and to use them to inspire you to do the work that must be done to bring your visions into reality.

Finding More Positives

Bringing positive energies into our lives, and into the lives of other people, requires us to think in a different direction than what we were used to.

I have been driving cars for 35 years, and not once has a policeman knocked on my door with a bunch of flowers to congratulate me for being so conscientious and careful.

That's the classic example of a society who thinks punishment long before we ever get to reward; where any positive attention has to be "earned" and is never freely given; where anything positive is rationed out like bowls of thin gruel to the endless lines of starving orphans ...

The energy body needs positive energies to function properly.

Exactly like the body needs proper food or **it <u>will</u> die**.

If we want people with strong energy bodies, we need to feed them properly, not starve them endlessly, withhold love, or punish them for failing to thrive.

That's just ... insane, if you think about it.

Next time you come across a stressed person, start asking yourself,

"What Positive does this person need?"

You don't need to say or do anything at this time, just ask yourself that question, often, for every person you meet (they are all way too stressed!) so you get into the swing of "thinking towards Positives."

With just a little practice, finding Positives becomes natural and easy again.

What Isn't This?

A great way of finding perfect Positives is to ask,

"What isn't this?"

We might be in a situation, and this situation is not:

- JOYFUL, FUN, EXCITING, INSPIRING, ENLIVENING, WONDERFUL, AMAZING, ENLIGHTENING.

Any of these will raise energy in the right way, in direct response to the situation you are in.

A person may be there, and they are definitely not:

- HAPPY, RADIANT, CONFIDENT, SUCCESSFUL, STRONG.

Any of these Positives are something they NEED in their lives, in their energy systems.

We can extend this to relationships and ask, "What isn't this family?"

- It's not HARMONIOUS, TOGETHER, LOVING, SUPPORTIVE.

Those are good energies to start with for the family entity (or the work team, or the young couple, or the mother and child team, the rock'n'roll band, the football squad etc.)

Finding Positives is something you get better at with practice and there is one more important thing to remember - with Positives, you can't go wrong.

The Right Positive

One of the most precious and delightful facts about Modern Energy Tapping is that you cannot go wrong with it.

**You can't ever give anyone, or yourself,
"the wrong positive."**

We can all do with more LOVE, JOY, HARMONY, CONNECTION, WEALTH, BEAUTY, RESPECT ...

We can all start to understand that there may well be no limit to just how good we can feel about ourselves, each other, people in general.

Our Plus Ten today may only be the beginning of the Plus Tens awaiting us as our energy systems recover from a lifetime of scurvy and start functioning as nature designed them to.

All Positives are simply aspects of love, and they are all precious and wonderful in their own right.

However, every time you do Modern Energy Tapping, there is the possibility that you might discover a magical Positive that unlocks your own energy system in a whole new way, just like the right key unlocks a door.

Actively seek for these personal, magical Positives.

You can find them far more easily when you are energy high.

Modern Energy Tapping is delightfully simply.

Start with the first Positive you need, right now, and then find the next one, the one after that ... until that threshold shift happens and your energy system comes to life in the most extraordinary way.

I encourage you strongly to start playing with the Positives when you are in a good mood and not wait until you are feeling bad to start energy tapping.

We can learn so much from getting ourselves into high energy states as often as possible!

Part 3 - From Problems To Solutions

"Problems are created in low energy states.
To solve problems, we need to be energy high!"
Silvia Hartmann

Solving Energy Body Problems

Modern Energy Tapping is for the energy body, to solve energy body problems.

There is no claim of cure for any physical, mental, or even spiritual (energy body based) problem.

What we do claim is that to improve energy flow through the energy body is the right thing to do.

- **Improving energy flow in the energy body creates change.**

We cannot predict exactly what this change will be.

People's energy systems are very individual, and interconnected.

At the baseline, Modern Energy is not here to heal the world of all disease or promise eternal youth.

- **Modern Energy, including Modern Energy Tapping, is designed to make people happier.**

It does this by addressing the energy component of any given problem.

The Energy Component

For any presenting problem, there may or may not be an energy component.

We do not know if a problem is an energy problem until we've energy tapped on it.

If there was a change, the problem did have an energy component.

If there was no change, this was not an energy problem and other ways to solve this problem must be sought.

This simple guideline keeps us clear, logical and safe.

The results of working especially with Positives can be stunning, amazing, can seem to be miraculous and inexplicable.

It is really as simple as to understand that problems have a sliding scale of the energy component from 0% to 100%.

For example, if a person has suffered for a long time from chronic pain and applies Modern Energy Tapping Positives, we cannot predict before we start what will happen.

It could be that nothing changes at all – the person is still in pain, in exactly the same way as they were before. This is incredibly rare as being in pain causes all manner of problems and additional stress beyond the physical sensations of pure pain, but it is conceivable that there is absolutely no change.

If that is the case, we can say that there was an energy component of 0% and the physical component is 100%. That is important to have known, learned and understood to plan the next step in solving this problem.

Another person with chronic pain starts tapping Positives, and the pain recedes somewhat, feels different, there was a small improvement.

Here, the energy component may have been around 15% and that is good to know. Even a small improvement is greeted with joy in this situation.

This sliding scale can go all the way to a person with severe chronic pain tapping Positives and finding that the pain is completely gone after the treatments.

In this case, the problem was 100% in the energy body in the first place.

- It is important to understand that we cannot know what the energy body component was until AFTER the treatment.

When we understand this, and explain this clearly to our clients if we are Modern Energy Professionals, all is well with the worlds.

We enter into a mode of investigation and research that is logical, reasonable and rational.

We begin to learn first hand just how important a part the energy body plays in the creation of our problems – and in the solutions.

The Artist

There was an artist who painted the same picture over and over again - a self portrait with a bleeding Christ on the cross forming eyebrows and nose. He had been painting the same picture for 20 years or more.

He was painting it yet again, stabbing violently at the canvas, when I walked in and said,

"You have been painting the problem for 20 years. Why don't you paint the solution?"

"How would I do that?" he asked incredulously.

"I don't know," I said, "If the solution had a colour, what colour would it be?"

His mouth fell open and then he shouted, "Blue! Blue! It would be blue!!!" and literally ran to get a fresh canvas.

He never painted that dreadful self portrait again ...

You Don't Have To Solve It, Only Evolve It!

Problems are really only problems when we feel "stuck" - it's not getting any better, we are not making any progress, and we might be losing hope that anything can be done.

Rome wasn't built in a day, and some problems require a lot of work and a long time before they have finally disappeared altogether.

What we need to look for is MOVEMENT.

- **We call this forward movement an EVOLUTION.**

It means that what we are doing is starting to work, we're on the right track, something is happening and the problem is not the same as it was when we started.

What we did HAD AN EFFECT.

As soon as that happens, all sorts of further positive side effects come into being.

We have hope again, and that's an energy rich state that allows us to do more and speed up the evolution of the problem.

The Solution Process: An Evolution Of Positives

We always start with what is needed the most, but that's not necessarily the end of the story.

For example, there was a gentleman who had severe money problems. He was about to lose his home and become essentially homeless and bankrupt, with nothing but debts and no resources remaining.

The situation had been building up for many years until it had become this bad but he felt "totally frozen and unable to do anything about it."

When offered to choose a first Positive for his dire situation, he chose PEACE.

The very first MET Sequence, simply asking for PEACE, made him much more peaceful and able to admit that the entire situation was his fault without becoming distraught or angry.

He was happier because he felt at peace with himself for the first time in years.

Although his financial situation had not changed yet, there had been a change - an evolution. A movement.

Even a small movement is a wonderful thing, the stalemate is broken, the spell is broken. Now, a process of solutions has begun, and that is why we say,

"You don't have to solve it, only evolve it!"

You keep evolving the situation and eventually, real practical change will manifest.

The next Positive our friend with the financial problems said he needed was STABILITY.

After that, he chose HOPE and then, ENERGY.

This progression was enough so he finally made an appointment with a charity which helps people in dire financial straights. This stabilised the situation and began the path out of the problem at last.

The First Positive

Now, consider a problem of your own that feels stuck.

Find a First Positive you need right now to get you started on that unfolding path from the problem to the eventual solution – and beyond.

Don't try to solve the entire problem all at once. That's like eating the proverbial elephant – often attempted but doomed to failure.

- **Think of one Positive that would make you feel better, right here, right now.**

What do you need? What do you want?

Assume the Heart Position, take three deep breaths in and out.

Then start energy tapping for the First Positive to begin the Solution Process.

The greatest journey begins with the first step.

The Next Positive

There is always a next Positive – which is for the new aspect the First Positive all over again.

- **Every aspect only has to think of their own First Positive.**

They do not have to worry about anything else. It is their job to say what they want most, feel they need the most, would help to make them happier.

In this way, we create a relay between the aspects, as one hands over responsibility for the next Positive to the new aspect.

And What Else ...?

People are so used to living in low energy states, they find it quite amazing to start feeling better after they have tapped for a Positive.

We have to learn just how good we can actually feel when our energy system really starts to wake up.

Add another sequence of Modern Energy Tapping, always, especially when you think you're done and you couldn't possibly feel any better.

Just ask,

- "And what else do I want more of in my life ..?"

- "What else would make this even better still ...?"

- "What else is there for me to want ...?"

- "How can I make this even better still?"

- "What else is there?"

- "How can I be even happier?"

Pick the next Positive, energy tap another sequence.

It's just energy, it's free and you can have all the energy you can allow yourself to want.

I Need A Miracle!

A wonderful and simple way to start on a track that can help you move forward in life is to evoke the power of the MIRACLE as your First Positive.

This is a very interesting energy experience which I recommend highly - try it out for yourself.

Think about something that you may have tried at one point but failed at, perhaps repeatedly; or something that other people can have, but for some reason, you can't ever achieve.

If you are really stuck with something completely impossible, use …

"Well that would take a MIRACLE!"

... as your First Positive.

Using the positive MIRACLE is particularly useful as a starter, to get us out of stuck places and get the energy moving.

With the energy moving, thoughts and ideas begin to flow as well, and you can really notice how using Modern Energy work can help us change our minds and our moods.

After you tapped a sequence of Modern Energy Tapping on MIRACLE, take a moment to reflect if what you wanted was really so impossible.

You might notice that you are now thinking differently; there may even be a glimmer of HOPE.

HOPE is a good step in the right direction; continue to either evolve the idea further, or pick new Positives until you feel really energized - and truly inspired, in the right sense of the word.

The Flowing Positives

A great way to improve the experience of Modern Energy Tapping is use your own words to let the Positives flow.

As you are tapping on each point, additional ideas and expansions on the original Positive come naturally into your mind.

Let your ideas flow to really own the Positives and make them meaningful and powerful for you.

Here is an example using the Positive VITALITY.

- Heart Position: I want more vitality in my life!

- Top of the head: Vitality - wake up my brain!

- Third eye point: Vitality - in every area of my life!

- Top of the eyebrow: Vitality - life energy!

- Corner of the eye: Vitality - make me strong!

- Under eye: Vitality - in every cell of my body!

- Under nose: Vitality - fresh, young energy!

- Under mouth: Vitality - glad to be alive!

- Collarbone: Vitality - God given vitality is alive inside of me!

- Thumb: Vitality - I want to share my vitality with my loved ones!

- Index finger: Vitality - Feel the force!

- Middle finger: Vitality - Sparks from my fingertips into all I do!

- Ring finger: Vitality - Comes to me so easily

- Little finger: Vitality - All the vitality in the world!

- Karate chop point: Vitality!!! Everything is alive and dances!!!

- Heart Position: I am so thankful for my vitality!

This is an example of what this one person came up with when they were tapping; when it is your own words, your own ideas, your own energy that flows, it is a wonderfully uplifting experience.

Try this now with a Positive that would be really helpful to.

Start with the three deep breaths in the Heart Position, then say whatever you want to say on each point as you tap. You can take as long as you want on each point when you are flowing Positives.

Do it now!

Finding Inspiration

The word "inspired" means "full of spirit" - and that's just another term for being filled with energy.

To solve problems, we need to be on top of our game.

When our energy flow becomes high, inspiration just happens naturally and as a side effect.

Once we are past needing a MIRACLE to even think about solving a problem, INSPIRATION is the next step.

What would inspire you particularly?

What energy positive might do the trick to catalyse you, bring you to life, wake you up, give you new, good ideas, like the veritable "Eureka!" lightning strike of inspiration?

It is particularly in inspiration that we find how our minds react to better energy flow in the energy body.

Ideas, insights and new solutions to old problems just start to flow, rush through our minds seemingly from nowhere, and it feels exciting, feels wonderful.

Whenever you are "stuck" with an intellectual challenge, a logical problem - and this can be an old personal problem just the same as a logistics problem, or a maths problem! - take a look at the Positives to help you find not only a solution, but an INSPIRED solution.

The world definitely needs many more of those!

The Mechanic

He said, "I feel stuck."

I said, "What kind of energy do you need to unstick yourself?

"Lubrication energy? Slippery energy? Slithery energy???"

He called out, "WD40 ENERGY!" - and we both fell about laughing.

When I asked how he felt after we had recovered from this laughing fit, he said, "Nope, definitely not feeling stuck any more! I know exactly what I'm supposed to do. And I'm going to do it – right now!"

He started laughing again and added, "And if I get stuck again, well, now I have my everlasting can of WD40 ENERGY!"

Solving Past Problems & Challenges

As we move through time, "we" become different people.

You are not the same person you were back then.

In order to make sure we understand this, we call past selves "past aspects" or just "aspects" for short.

Instead of saying, "I did a terrible thing in 1993," we say, "An aspect did a terrible thing in 1993 ..."

As soon as we do this, we gain a much better perspective on what happened, and why it happened.

We can heal past injuries of an energetic nature by "sending positive energy to that past aspect" who needed help but didn't have it at the time.

So the question we ask is:

"What can I send to my past aspect today that would have helped at the time?"

This may be something like ...

⭐ LOGIC if the past aspect did something very stupid; or

⭐ LOVE if the past aspect was unloved;

⭐ HAPPINESS if the past aspect was terribly unhappy, or

⭐ SERENITY if the aspect was stressed out of their minds;

⭐ ANGEL ENERGY for a desperate aspect;

⭐ FORGIVENESS ENERGY for an aspect who made a mistake;

⭐ ... ENERGY for an aspect of your own ...?

When we do this, we - right here, right now - overcome that problem and reconnect with our own aspects over time.

We are healing and energizing the past aspect.

This makes us stronger and happier HERE AND NOW.

Here and now is the only place of power,

from where we get to shape our futures.

Solving Future Problems & Challenges

Many of us are highly stressed not because our lives are bad at the moment, but because we are afraid of something bad that will happen in the future.

Naturally, we try not to think about problems in the future and "take our minds off it" by trying to distract ourselves with busywork, social media, playing computer games, watching TV and a myriad of other ways, but it doesn't work - the stress is ever present in the energy system, even if we are good at ignoring it.

Using Modern Energy Tapping is a great way to end these future fears and worries.

Think about your future self, the future aspect who will have to face that problem.

What energies would he or she need to deal with the problem?

Focus on the future aspect as you tap the first Positive, then pick another, and another, until you can really feel that fear lifting and being replaced by a sense of strength and confidence, right here and now.

By doing this, you are changing the future for real - because you are changing the present you, right here and now.

It's a fascinating thing ...

Here is an example how to work with a future aspect and to deal with fears about the future.

An older lady is terrified of having to go into a nursing home. She imagines a future aspect, lonely, scared, cold, hungry and in pain, in a dingy bed in the dark.

> ✴ **What gifts of energy can we send this poor future aspect so she will feel a little better, happier, stronger?**

The lady here and now wanted to send LIGHT as the First Positive.

She assumed the Heart Position and said, "I send you LIGHT."

She repeated this on the energy tapping points and when the sequence was complete, in the Heart Position, she sighed deeply and started to relax a little.

The next Positive she chose was CARE, then LOVE, then "the love of God and the Angels."

At the end, the future aspect was in a bright and comfortable place, being well cared for by kind people, but there were also angels nearby and the room was filled with love.

The lady in question reported that she had had her first good night's sleep in many years following this treatment, and this has remained the case until now.

Using Positives With Health Challenges

We cannot repair our bodies with modern energy work, but we can help our bodies be stronger and most importantly, remove stress and emotional disturbances through Modern Energy Tapping.

Energy Tapping for Positives that you feel you need every day is a good beginning; but we can be more specific than that.

If a particular body part is affected, we can send it something it needs to feel better, just as we did with the past and future aspects.

Here are some examples of how this works.

- A little girl with a congenital eye disease energy tapped for "Happy eyes."

- A man who had broken his ankle energy tapped for "Strong bones."

- A lady who had cancer energy tapped for TIME; as a result, she became "unfrozen" and found the energy to make the most of the time she had remaining.

- An older lady with thyroid disease energy tapped for TENDERNESS.

- A man who had suffered a heart attack energy tapped for "My loving heart."

- A man who had stomach ulcers energy tapped for SERENITY.

Focus on the body part that is in trouble and ask what you can send it as a gift, to make it feel better, to make it stronger, happier.

It feels amazing and the more you do it, the better your results in mind, body and spirit will become.

Ending The War On Disease

First, the disclaimer – we make no claim of cure for physical disease.

Modern Energy Tapping is for the energy body.

The energy body does not respond well to being at war with anything.

A strong, powerful energy body can help the physical body work better and that is extremely important in any healing process.

When we work with the energy of healing, we don't engage in a war.

We use positive energy – the power of love.

We ask, "What does my energy body need to be strong and powerful?"

Find the First Positive and start from there.

Keep your energy body strong.

Heart Healing

⭐ **The Heart of Energy is the power centre of the energy body.**

When a person suffers from a broken heart, the entire energy system goes down and their energy body will go into chronic stress. The person will be permanently low on the Energy Chart, and it is simply impossible to do anything right, or to be successful at anything at all, with a broken heart.

The worse the problems are, and the longer a person has suffered, the more important it becomes to literally start with the heart.

In the Heart Position, we place our own Healing Hands of Energy on our own Heart of Energy.

Even when we are very low on energy, this stabilises the energy heart.

Holding the Heart Position and breathing deeply gives us the space to think of a first Positive.

- What do you want to give to your own dear Heart of Energy, here and now?

- What do you wish would come, would be, would happen to start healing your heart?

This is a very personal, very moving way of working with gentle Positives, one at a time.

If you or someone else has suffered from serious heart break and is suffering still, I recommend to do this three times a day, for at least nine days, morning, noon and before going to sleep at night, in the same way a person would take prescription medicine.

When the Heart of Energy comes back online, the entire energy body reacts with renewed strength, vitality and vigour.

Also, under high stress and at any time, to take care of the Heart of Energy is the best way to stabilise yourself and start moving forward into more personal power, health, and happiness.

Part 4 - Modern Energy Tapping For Two - And More!

"The more energy we have, the more connected we become."

Silvia Hartmann

Modern Energy Tapping Together

Modern Energy Tapping for and by ourselves is wonderful, but it gets so much better when you tap with one or more other people.

There are lots of applications for tapping Positives together and at the same time.

For example:

- When a person is ill, upset or stressed

- Energy Tapping with a child

- Energy Tapping for something both or all of you want in your shared lives or work together.

The simple question we ask is:

What would make you/us feel much better?

There are variations on this question, such as:

- What would make you feel better about that problem you have (at school)?

- What would make this team perform much better?

- What does this company need to get into profit?

- What does this family need to be much happier?

- What do you need so you can feel better?

- What do you/we need to have more success?

- What can we send to (x) to help them right now?

- What isn't this situation like at all?

As always, we can choose from the list of Positives if nothing comes to mind and start with that.

Once the energy starts moving, people will have their own ideas of what to say and do next. If in doubt, simply run with the MORE ENERGY! pattern, or let them choose a new Positive from the list for the next sequence.

Be Light Hearted!

The first rule of Modern Energy Tapping with other people is to be light-hearted about it.

Energy is light in nature, and when we get too serious, that's a sign of blocked energy flow.

Modern Energy Tapping is a happy, light thing, a light filled, energizing adventure; if you offer it like that, other people will be happy to give it a go.

Remember this:

⭐ **There isn't a person in the world who doesn't want to feel better!**

That's an absolute fact, and by offering people the list of Positives to choose from, most people you will ever meet will be more than happy to give it a go, try it out for themselves.

As you tap a sequence of Positives with another person or a group, look for the following signs that they are getting less stressed and their energy flow is starting to improve:

- They relax

- They might start to smile

- They might start to comment on how they are feeling

- They might start to move

- They might breathe more deeply.

If you notice any of these things, tell your person/s what you have noticed and that you are happy they are starting to relax and come to life. Modern Energy Tapping is working!

Allow yourself to get excited too, you are a part of this experience and you are having your own experiences as you tap along with others.

This is what makes Modern Energy Tapping really exciting and enlivening as a facilitator, helper, or friend, lover or parent.

We get to share in other people's happiness.

Energy Tapping With A Friend

The exciting part about tapping with a friend is that you can take turns at choosing Positives.

This often results on both getting to tap for Positives they would not have chosen themselves.

Also, as you go through the points, you can share ideas and insights, encourage one another and bring the energy higher between you.

 An important note:

Even if you are "helping a friend in need" please allow yourself to get into it and enjoy the Positive yourself as well.

Modern Energy Tapping works best when you are engaged and having a good experience yourself. Allow yourself to want the Positive to come into your life too; this creates a powerful double-pull and increases the energy flow and the enjoyment.

Remember that high energy states are about feeling really happy, laughing, dancing around the room, feeling fully alive and delighted.

And don't forget to congratulate each other on a job well done at the end!

Changing Other People With The Energy Gift

Often, our problems are not our problems, but other people's problems which affect us directly.

A stroppy teenage daughter, a friend in crisis, a stressed partner, a difficult boss, an ailing parent – other people's problems can have a huge impact on our own energy states, on our happiness.

With Modern Energy, we can do something about it.

- **We can send other people a gift of energy, a blessing.**

This has two results.

Often, you will notice that the person behaves differently after this has been done.

This is not magic, it happens because at the energy levels we are much more connected than we realise. Energy travels around freely between people, that is why we are affected by the emotions of other people.

The second result of sending a positive energy gift to another person, or an aspect of another person, is that you will feel different in the here and now.

Whether you were annoyed or worried, angry or sad, freaked out or stressed, you now feel much better in yourself. This is always very welcome and puts you in a much better position to deal with problems more sensibly, more pro-actively and more successfully.

This is how you give the gift of positive energy.

1. Think of the person, or a particular aspect of that person, and find a Positive that would make them happier.

2. Assume the Heart Position, take three deep breaths in and out and then state clearly, "I give the gift of (ENERGY) to Peter."

3. On each point, you say, "(ENERGY)for Peter."

Finish with the Heart Position as usual.

This is a lovely thing to do and allows us to send much needed positive energy to any aspect of any person across time and space.

Energy Tapping For A Relationship

Two people who are in a relationship can choose Positives that would enhance the relationship itself.

A relationship is more than the sum of its parts.

- "What does this relationship need, right now?"

- "What isn't this relationship at the moment?"

- "What can we give to this relationship to heal it?"

- "What would make our relationship even better?"

- "What would add extra sparkle to our relationship?"

- "What would make our relationship even more exciting?"

- "What good quality our relationship already has shall we energize even more?"

Focusing on positive energies and tapping together, choosing Positives together or taking it in turn to choose a positive creates a powerful bond and strengthens relationships on the energetic level.

Energy Tapping For A Team Or A Group

A team can be a sports team, a group of co-workers, the managers in a company, a band, a class of students and their teacher or any get-together of different people who are working together on common aims.

With Modern Energy Tapping, we absolutely focus on those common aims and consider what kind of energy would make it so much easier and more effortless to achieve these aims.

The key is to improve the energy flow in the team by raising the energy flow of the members of the team.

A sequence of Modern Energy Tapping does not take very long; with smaller teams, individuals can pick their favourite Positives one at a time and everyone taps them together and at the same time.

Often, the common aim gives a good clue which positive to choose, for example:

- "This team needs more SUCCESS!"

- "This band needs more HARMONY."

- "This family needs to PLAY more often."

For large groups or teams which have very individual members, a simple way of improving everyone's energy flow is to let the individuals choose their own Positive, and then let the whole group tap together on

"My Positive!"

or

"My ENERGY."

Energy Tapping Positives In A Family

Getting the whole family together to tap for Positives is an amazing bonding experience.

Everyone can join in, even children as young as two years of age.

Everyone can add their thoughts and their wishes, and everyone can have fun with this.

It's perfectly alright to be playful - indeed, that is the best way to work with the Positives, and the best way to lighten up and improve the energy flow in each member of the family.

As each family member begins to sparkle and shine, the connections between them become stronger and the "family field" as a whole becomes more aligned, more powerful, more supportive and more empowering.

Modern Energy Tapping can be done around the dinner table, but also as a game on a car journey, on a rainy day or at any time the family needs to lighten up, pull together and find laughter, fun and love in each other's company.

If this is not possible, a single person can tap for the "family entity" and consider what they would like to make it happier.

It is very interesting how the changes transmit through the family field and other individuals respond to this - even if they did not tap themselves, or even knew that someone did.

Energy Tapping Positives With Children

Young children love to play with energy and they love to feel good; Modern Energy Tapping is a wonderful game that can make an enormous difference to a child's life from the moment he or she learns that there are simple ways to take control of one's emotions.

As ABUNDANCE and GRACE and their ilk are a little beyond children conceptually, a simple way to make it fun and interesting is to invite the child to use a magical power, or a super power such as:

Flying	Super Speed	X-Ray Vision
Rainbow Hands	Talking To Animals	Fairy Magic
Fire Breathing	Shape Shifting	Invisible
Princess Power	Bullet Proof	Mermaid Magic
Super Strength	Hero Power	Super Smart
Brave	Jedi Power	Wizard Power
Mind Reading	Being Bendy	Super Hearing

Children are very much in tune with their energy states, much more so than adults. They also have a much better grasp on what they want and their imagination is still alive, so simply talking to a child and asking them what they might like in the way of extra "powers" for life will produce delightful, surprising results and will be perfect for the child in question.

When we think, talk and feel, all things are only energy.

We can ask a child, what would make you happy, right now?

The child might answer with, "A car!"

At this point, the car is only energy.

By allowing this energy to flow in, through and out, by tapping for "a car" we are giving this child something that money cannot buy and we will always end up smiling and a lot happier than we were before.

Hero Energy

For teenagers but also for many adults, personal heroes are one of the greatest sources of inspiration and strength.

To aspire to align with Hero Energy is a wonderful thing for boys and girls of all ages, and using a person or a fictional character as the metaphor for the kind of energy which inspires works amazingly well.

Modern Energy Tapping using the name of the hero or heroine is a powerfully uplifting energy experience.

- Who are your own personal heroes and heroines?

- Who has inspired you, dead, alive or imaginary?

- Who do you want to be like "when you grow up"?

- And if you are in trouble, which hero could help you with their energy right now?

You can tap for the hero's name or simply add ENERGY to the person of your choice.

This is a simple and wonderful way to use the energy of people to empower your life.

I want more ...

- Mother Theresa ENERGY

- Superman ENERGY

- Gandhi ENERGY

- Richard The Lionheart ENERGY

- Branson ENERGY

- (Name of my lover) ENERGY

Pick a person who inspires you and try this. It's a unique experience, there's nothing quite like it.

Part 5 - Modern Energy Basics

"Love without logic is insanity. And vice versa."
Silvia Hartmann

The 6th Sense

*Do you know that feeling when your stomach is churning,
or when your hands are cold and trembling?*

When your back and neck feels all locked up and tight?

When there's a pressure on your chest and you can't breathe?

That's what other people call "emotions"!!!

We cannot see energy, but we can feel energy in our bodies.

The 6th Sense are the sensations of energy as it moves through our energy body.

We feel empowered when these sensations are electric, tingling, fast and it makes us feel alive, young and strong.

We feel depressed and weak when these sensations are missing, or dull, heavy or even painful.

Emotions are not in the mind.

Emotions are feelings in the body - the sensations of the energy body.

These 6th Sense sensations range from very fine sensations, such as a light shiver when entering into a room with a strange atmosphere, via what we think of as emotions, all the way to sensations that are so strong, they have become indistinguishable from physical pain. Those are called psychosomatic emotions.

Intuition ← Emotion ← Psychosomatic Pain/Pleasure

Those are simply escalations on a single scale of 6th Sense sensations.

It was never understood properly what we have to do to "feel better."

To put it simply, we need to look after the energy body more.

The first thing the energy body needs is proper food - it needs HEALTHY energy to come in as often as possible for all its functions.

Our 6th Sense is designed to let us know when we NEED some energy food.

Unfortunately, we have been societally entrained to ignore our intuition.

Men especially have also been trained to ignore the stronger sensations of emotions, and many don't even become aware of the feedback from the energy body until the situation has become critical and energy body stress causes intense symptoms.

By becoming aware of the situation, and then starting to feed the energy body with the kind of energy it needs to work better again, we are doing the right thing.

It is quite simple but it demands that instead of endlessly reporting our problems, we start to think in terms of SOLUTIONS instead.

Future Orientation

Looking back at the traumas of the past has been the navel gazing fascination of psychoanalysis for the past hundred years.

Modern energy work shows us that this is an unhealthy thing to be doing, as it ties the energy body into knots.

The energy body is a natural system that wants to move forward, flow forward as all things do in nature; and in a very practical way, there is nothing any of us can do to change the past.

- **We only have the NOW, and then, the FUTURE, to add new and different experiences to our lives.**

The Criminal

I had a client some time ago, a young man who was found at age 6 approximately in a warehouse which had been used by a paedophile ring to make movies.

He was put into care, given a name and birthday as his own was not known, and later adopted by a rich couple. When he became too difficult with the onset of puberty, he was sent back into care; he was abused there too so he ran away. To survive, he then became a prostitute, drug addict and criminal and spent most of his time in and out of prison.

He told me his story in broad brushstrokes, told me about his problems and then asked me, "Can you make me normal?"

I thought about it and then said, "No. Not a chance in hell."

He nodded, laughed and said, "Thank God, at least you're honest ..."

Then, he asked, "So what am I to do?"

And I could feel that energy rising and I said to him,

"You make sure you have the best life now. The best experiences. Make your life count for something. Pack in as many moments of joy, of grace, of pure happiness as you can.

"Then there has to come a time when the Positives outweigh the negatives, and you will have had an amazing life when all is said and done."

So and instead of delving into any of his innumerable traumas and bad memories, we started working with Positives. To begin with, what he was already good at, what he was proud of. His sensitivity, intelligence, creativity. His strength and the fact that he had never given up. It was an awesome session and he left inspired, delighted, and proud of himself.

It was so simple too. In moments of crisis, he would find a Positive to lift him as he had seen the Energy Chart and understood that he was not "irreparably damaged" but instead, highly stressed all the time, and so life got better for him - of course it did.

Will he ever need to re-visit any of the terrible memories?

Who knows?

That was his past life, and now his life is different.

He is evolving.

As we all are.

What is it you want to achieve in your life?

Focus on that.

What do you need right HERE AND NOW to get you to that, to help you achieve that?

Call that energy in and use it to empower you.

Keep yourself strong in the NOW and focus on the future YOU WANT.

- **There is only energy, and the absence of energy.**

Don't take my word for it, try it for yourself.

Normal people don't need psychoanalysis.

Normal people need to de-stress and start to feel strong, happy, and loved inside.

When that happens, what seemed to be a mountain becomes a molehill and we can get on with what's really important - our own lives and to shape them in the creation of our own personal happiness.

Evoking Energy

Modern Energy Tapping is only the beginning.

By paying attention to our 6th Sense and particularly, on what it feels like when we are getting stressed, we are learning to use a natural system that belongs to us and which has more than a thousand and one uses in every day life.

Remember that there is only energy, and the absence of energy.

As we pay attention to our 6th Sense sensations, we also become aware when we are in the presence of nourishing, helpful, incoming energies.

We learn to let in more energy - from the sky, from the sunshine, from wind and rain, from people, from the world around us.

People who have started Modern Energy Tapping have reported that often, they just need to think of a particular Positive and they can already feel the energy rising, without even having to tap for it.

There is a progression in our ability to regulate our own energy systems of which energy tapping is just the very first start, much like singing the Alphabet song is a very first start to learning to read and write.

We all have to start somewhere, and the practice of Modern Energy Tapping is an easy and simple way to help our energy bodies become healthier and stronger.

The more you energy tap, the sooner you'll learn how to improve your energy levels without having to tap at all.

Learning how energy works for you is what it's all about at the end of the day.

How Much Pleasure Can You Stand?

How many times a day do you think tapping a sequence of Modern Energy Tapping would be good for you?

Three?

Five?

A sequence of Modern Energy Tapping only takes about two minutes ...

It is interesting to note that we are so used to feeling relatively miserable and uninspired in daily life that we can hardly imagine what it would be like to really have lots of energy and feel happy anyway - even if we're not on holiday or at a party or in meditation.

I would strongly, strongly encourage you to add some Modern Energy Tapping to your boring or dreary routines, be they data entry or dish washing, painting houses or screwing the feet on a fridge in a production line for 8 hours a day.

"What Positive could make me happier, right here, right now?"

That's the question we should ask all the time - because I don't think there's any kind of ceiling on how happy we can be.

Even if our material circumstances didn't change at all.

That's the true magic of modern energy endeavours - by taking control of our energy systems, we cut out the middle man and get to have experiences even if we are not rich, young, or beautiful.

You can be happy, whatever the weather.

That is true personal freedom and has to lead to new paths and new unfoldments for you in the long run.

Ask for more.

And even more.

And then, all the rest as well.

In the energy worlds, we can have it all, and have it right now!

Modern Energy Tapping – And Beyond!

"If you fill your mind to overflowing with beautiful things,
there can be no room left for doubt."

Silvia Hartmann

In this manual, you have found many ideas, instructions, exercises, examples and suggestions how to raise energy by Modern Energy Tapping – activating the awesome Power of the Positives.

Modern Energy Tapping is a wonderful thing and it can work wonders.

What it does most of all is to correct an old piece of destructive brainwashing - namely that you have to re-live your darkest moments in order to be free of them.

This has caused a dangerous fixation on the past, and on judging, apportioning blame, getting endlessly entangled with the past, thereby dragging the past into the present to a degree which has become unhealthy and even a serious cause for problems in its own right.

With a clear future orientation, less stress in the energy body and the ability to feel REALLY REALLY GOOD, any time you choose to do so, we are on the other side of a paradigm shift.

We need to re-draw the maps of the cause and effect of human behaviour.

Also, we need to celebrate.

To have had a good life, you will need as many GOOD experiences as possible in every single day.

Modern Energy Tapping helps us remember how good we can feel, and then takes us into good feelings we have never felt before!

That's exciting, that's inspiring and that's what the stressed world of men needs right now.

Modern Energy Tapping relies on the Power of the Positives to make groundbreaking changes in the way we think, we feel and we act.

This requires a different way of thinking about all our problems.

It represents a solutions-based approach that includes the energy body as an absolute factor in our living realities.

Modern Energy Tapping is an easy way to try out the real blessings of working with Positives, with positive energy.

It is a simple introduction and allows us to access the Oceans of Energy at will. Yet, MET is only the beginning.

Once we have understood the cause and effect of energy in our lives, we can apply this newfound knowledge in all manner of ways to improve the quality of our lives.

This is the aim and the goal of Modern Energy – to make people happier.

Happier people, people who are filled with energy and have energy to give to their loved ones, their friends, their communities and humanity at large is exactly what we all need.

Every one of us who becomes happier, becomes more empowered, is a gift to us all.

The Positives are a portal to a different way of being. They are uplifting, inspiring, healing. They are the step stones to a very different future.

Learn how to raise energy.

Live life.

Feel POWERFULLY.

Be alive.

And most of all, make it your business to be as happy as possible.

With all my best blessings,

Silvia Hartmann

December 10th, 2017

Part 6 - The Love Challenge

"You find yourself at +10."
Silvia Hartmann

Introduction To The Love Challenge

In 2011, I spoke before the GoE Energy Conference and begged the participants to come out of the energy closet.

Then, it was thought that if you talked about energy, you would have to be a fool. People were afraid to admit that they were working with energy, reversed to stand up and speak their truth.

I taught the participants to hold out their hands and to say,

"Good morning! My name is ... and I am a Modern Energist!"

"I specialise in human emotions and particularly, Modern Stress Management."

It helps that the Modern Energy Theory I have created is not only reasonable and rational, but also makes sense to every normal human being on this planet.

Coming out of the energy closet and not only admitting that we are Modern Energists was the first step.

Since then, many years have passed and we have successfully navigated the energy challenge.

The next challenge is here – the Love Challenge.

In order to understand the origins of the Love Challenge, we have to travel back to 1993, where a past aspect was researching animal behaviour, and in particular, the so called "Rage Syndrome."

The day came, and the aspect had a breakthrough experience and understood that the problem was all about love.

Rage Syndrome in social mammals is caused by an absence of love.

There is a very real energy exchange going on between social mammals, and when this energy exchange is disturbed or disrupted, terrible things happen.

Terrible, terrible things.

There was a study about orphans back in the day, where nurses were allowed to feed and change orphaned babies, but they were not allowed to interact with them beyond that. No eye contact, the nurses wore gloves and did not speak.

What happened after a time was that the babies stopped crying. Then they stopped eating, and then they started dying.

At which point the nurses, even back then, refused to take further part and so the experiment was never completed.

This energy exchange between social mammals is a structural occurrence and not limited to people. These energy exchanges happen between horses, monkeys, dolphins, cats, dogs, rats, elephants, meerkats and lions.

All the social mammals have these energy exchanges happening between them, and these energy exchanges are absolutely crucial to their intelligence, their social functioning, their physical health, their powers of recovery, to their emotional health, to their behaviour, how they react in any given environment and how they behave with each other.

In a flash, my aspect saw the effects of lack of love on social mammals.

Yes, and there is the story of how my 1993 aspect ran into the room with the animal behaviour library, which contained everything that had ever been published in the English language on animal behaviour, every book, every scientific study. She took one book after the other from the shelf and looked through them, but the word LOVE wasn't in any of them.

Not one occurrence, not in any of them.

There was a mountain of scientific books at the aspect's feet, and the word LOVE was not in any of them.

That is where I come from – to bring LOVE back into science.

All the various things I've done over the decades have never been only about tapping, or EMO, or any of that.

The core drive is to re-combine LOVE and LOGIC.

It is of the essence to bring love into science because without it, you cannot understand people.

You cannot make sense of people at all without factoring in emotions.

Further, people themselves cannot make sense of the Universe at large without factoring in emotions.

Yes, and so I brought down this whole story to emotions being feedback devices from the energy body.

When the energy body is happy, we experience happy emotions.

When the energy body is unhappy or in pain, we experience negative emotions.

From EMO we know that the exact place where we feel our emotional pain is the exact place where the disturbance in the energy body is located.

"Where do you feel this heartbreak in your body? Show me with your hands!"

We don't have to guess, we don't have to intuit, people can show us where it hurts, and that's the place that needs healing.

We can put our healing hands of energy over that place and find out what happens next …

When we take the energy body seriously, all of a sudden emotions make sense. They become structural, systemic, and predictable. We have a science of energy – The Third Field.

Going back to the original desire to bring love back into science, of course it was all about love. That was the word the aspects used. But then they got involved in the New Age, and the aspects changed their terminology to be less offensive – instead of love, we talked about energy.

We are "The Guild of Energists" not "The Guild of Lovers."

This might change in the future, especially now that we have The Energy of Attraction.

Now, to the Love Challenge.

The State Of Play

The world of men is a mess – and it's not getting any better.

Wherever you look, there is a nightmare unfolding that destroys human lives in any way you might want to conceive of it.

The problems are so many, so grandiose, so intense, they are frightening and overwhelming.

In the picture above, we see a little brown child looking at a burning heap of garbage.

In the so-called civilised world, we live in the illusion that things are getting better. We live in our clean cities with street lights and spend our time sending each other motivational pictures on social media. Every year, a new E-Phone comes out and we can celebrate that – it's progress.

Things are getting better …

No, they are not getting better - and there is one particular topic that breaks into that illusion of the modern world.

The Trillion Dollar Stress Pandemic

The so-called civilised world is breaking down under the chronic stress of its inhabitants.

For all the yoga, consumption of organic foods, recycling and wearing exercise watches that tell us how many steps we've walked today, stress is rising and rising – and so is the cost of stress.

Here is something that cannot be ignored any longer, because it is starting to hit the illusion where it hurts – in the accumulation of profits.

To be sure, the Trillion Dollar Stress Pandemic isn't nearly as expensive as all the money spent on the tools and toys of war. It is a drop in the ocean compared to that.

The problem is however that the stress problem is personal. People have real experience of it, what it does to their lives. Stress is not as easily ignored as wars fought far away in foreign countries, or little brown children looking at the destruction of their environments.

Stress is a real problem and there is no solution to be found in the illusionary non-reality of the world of men.

The Mysterious Energy Body

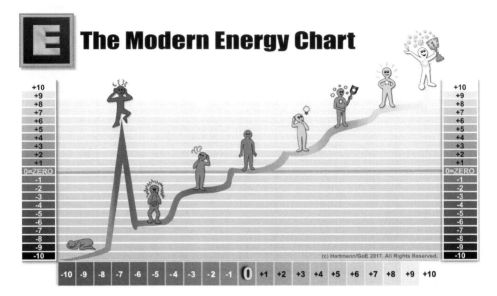

As Modern Energists, we have an entire set of new theories, methodologies and techniques to address stress in a whole new way.

This is a proven and effective way; we've been doing this for 25 years now and we know that it works.

It all starts with the idea, "YES! You really have an energy body!"

Followed by, "And NO, it's not that wibbly wobbly thing from energy medicine, that is so abstract that you have to meditate and see auras and lick flowers.

"NO! I am not talking about some sort of subtle energy body.

"I'm talking about the energy body that makes a man punch his wife in the face and knock her teeth out.

"I'm talking about the sort of energy body that makes a person jump off a motorway bridge, because they can't stand the pain of living any longer, and cause an accident that kills six hundred people, including a school bus full of kids.

"That's the sort of energy body I'm talking about!"

People hear this and are astonished.

130

They say, "What you mean a real energy body?"

I say, "Yes. A real energy body. With an energy head, and energy organs, and healing hands of energy!

"That real energy body expresses itself in emotions, and depending on how well the energy body functions, how high or low your energy body states are, is not only how you feel, and how you act, but also what structural grammar you are using in your language; what beliefs you hold, and those are different between the different energy body states, and your entire physical body chemistry changes as well."

The Modern Energy Chart gives us an overview of the different energy body states we can inhabit, from -10 to +10. The fact is that every normal human being will have been in all of these states at some point in their lives, no matter how briefly.

We have had aspects that were on top of the world; we have had aspects who succeeded. We have also had aspects who were so broken down, they lay down on the floor and cried.

We have had aspects who were truly terrified; aspects who questioned themselves.

We have been bored and lifeless, uninspired and grey.

We have had aspects who had good ideas, and we have had aspects who went out to work on a project, full of excitement and energy.

This is good and right. I do not believe that we're supposed to be floating around locked into a constant state of +10 all the time. Human experience covers the range and makes us real, makes us wise. The most fertile landscapes exist where the weather changes, where there is sunshine and rain, thunderstorms and blue skies – all of it.

So essentially, we want to embrace the entire range of human experiences, but there is a problem.

The problem is that we do not have nearly enough good experiences on the plus side of the Energy Chart.

This is curious, as every human being lives and strives all the time for better experiences, better emotions.

It is also a question that has troubled me deeply for quite some time now.

The Evil Scissors

I said in conversation not long ago that it seemed to me that at some point, someone came along with a great big pair of evil scissors, cut that scale in half - and then threw the good half away!

All we're left with is that crazy negative side.

For example, here is a pain assessment tool from medical practice.

The Pain Assessment Tool

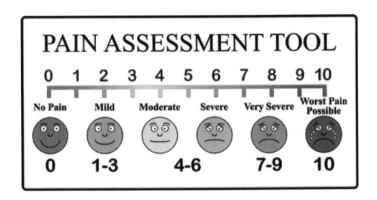

It goes from 10, what we would call -10, and ends at ZERO – no pain.

This scale is missing the positive side altogether.

Surely, beyond simply feeling no pain, feeling nothing, there is more to be had?

Shouldn't there be a state where the body feels good, then great, then spectacular – and THAT is the truly healed state?

Are people sent home way too early in medical treatments, halfway through, without a real healing ever having been reached ..?

The SUD Scale

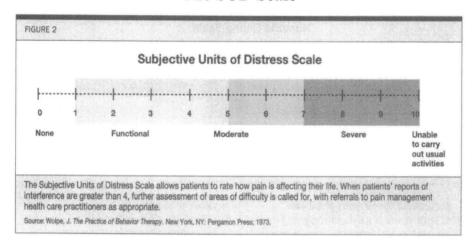

FIGURE 2

Subjective Units of Distress Scale

| 0 | 1 | 2 | 3 | 4 | 5 | 6 | 7 | 8 | 9 | 10 |

None   Functional   Moderate   Severe   Unable to carry out usual activities

The Subjective Units of Distress Scale allows patients to rate how pain is affecting their life. When patients' reports of interference are greater than 4, further assessment of areas of difficulty is called for, with referrals to pain management health care practitioners as appropriate.

Source: Wolpe, J. The Practice of Behavior Therapy. New York, NY: Pergamon Press; 1973.

And then we have the Subjective Units of Distress scale (SUD Scale), a psychology instrument clearly copied straight across from the medical pain scale.

Again, we are only measuring pain, and we're not measuring pleasure here.

Indeed, exactly as with the medical pain chart, the positive side of this scale is simply absent.

It isn't there. It doesn't exist at all. This is a conceptual nightmare.

Medicine might get away with it, but to try and understand people this is blatantly a pack of cards with all the trumps removed.

When I started to work with people, I asked them a question nobody else had asked. I would ask a sex abuse victim, "So what was good about it?"

They would be astonished and taken aback, but I would ask again, "What was good about it?"

And the person might say, "Well, there was the ice cream and feeling special. And most of all, knowing more than all the other children. They knew nothing, but I knew everything."

Now, we have a bigger picture. Now, we know more than we did before that question was asked. We have more information than we did when we only asked about the pain.

This was when I found the Guiding Stars, the high positive experiences that cause a person to repeat the same behaviours over and over again.

The classic example is that of a boy who sees his mother's high heeled shoe, has his first sexual experience and now he's a shoe collector, age 43, with 123,000 pairs of high heeled shoes. He has no wife, no love life, no life at all, no friends, but he has shoes – and it comes straight from that one highly positive experience.

Unless you understand both trauma and Guiding Star, you can never understand a person as there is an interplay between positive and negative experiences.

Yerkes Dobson Law Of Arousal

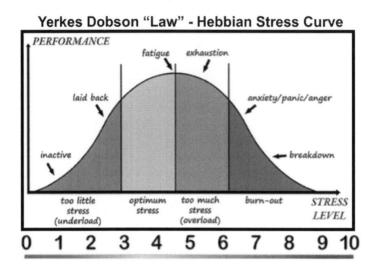

Yerkes Dobson "Law" - Hebbian Stress Curve

Here is a third example of that missing positive side of the Energy Chart.

When I was writing the Modern Stress Management materials, I decided to have a look what the current standard of Stress Research might be at, and I found "The Yerkes Dobson LAW of Arousal."

Here, we have two American scientists in 1908 and their rats.

These guys had a sleeping rat in a cage, and then they would electro-shock it and open a door to a maze, and then measure how long it took for the rat to get to the end of the maze. If they didn't shock the rat enough, the rat would go back to sleep. If they shocked the rat too much, it would freak out completely and throw itself around like a lunatic, and that would be our -7, where the Rage Syndrome was found.

If they shocked the rats just enough, the rat would wake up in a panic and try to run away as fast as it could in sheer terror.

From this our friends Yerkes and Dobson created THE LAW OF AROUSAL.

The LAW. Of AROUSAL. 1908. On this scientific basis, people have been stressing their workers, their soldiers, their school children and presumably their scientists, to drive them into what they called optimal stress – which is actually our -4 and -5 stress, and what we call severe and debilitating chronic stress.

What Yerkes and Dobson failed to do was to let the rats have a good night's sleep, and let them wake up naturally. To give them a good breakfast – and then put a female rat at the end of that maze. They never did that experiment, but I guarantee that those happy rats would have produced better results in terms of learning the maze, the speed and elegance of their movements and how fast they would get there, reliably, every single time.

There is a pattern here that is is deeply disturbing.

The Wall At ZERO

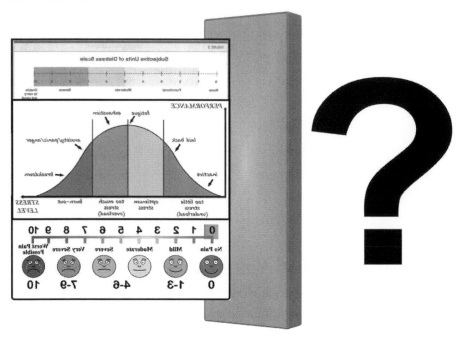

The pattern that is being revealed here is that there is a gigantic barrier at ZERO.

This barrier keeps people trapped on the wrong side of the Energy Chart.

This is a conceptual prison - the good stuff isn't there, doesn't even exist conceptually.

Nobody is looking beyond ZERO, nobody is researching beyond ZERO, and this has some truly nasty repercussions for humanity at large.

War, Peace, ...???

War and peace are a perfect example. War is obviously the -7 state when entire groups or whole civilisations completely lose the plot and starting to mindlessly and senselessly attack each other.

But what is peace? What are the ideas or internal representations of peace?

It's usually a bunch of farmers labouring away in their fields, or some vegan happy family eating vegetables round a big table in the countryside somewhere.

A true ZERO state where nothing is gained, nothing is achieved, where there is no evolution and looking forward to digging for our turnips until the day we die is the best a man can get.

This is extremely unattractive as a goal in and of itself, but it gets worse.

The balance point between war and that kind of peace is, please note, at -4, the exact same place where Yerkes and Dobson had their stressed rats trying to escape the terror, and on the energy body chart, the place where self doubt turns into fear and paranoia.

It's little wonder that we have so much war, are always on the brink of war!

A true balance would require that other side of the chart being present, but of course, it isn't there.

Peace is the ZERO point of nothing. If you want to end war, you don't need peace as a goal. You need a much higher goal. Essentially, you need love as the goal. When you fall short of that, at least we might be on the right side of the chart and can come up with some creative, practical solutions to the problems that caused the wars in the first place.

The second example is that of the eternal fight between good and evil, in the diagram represented by SuperMan and some random -7 nemesis, some angry guy who wants to destroy everything, which is the hallmark of the -7 state of senseless, random violence and mindless revenge.

SuperMan has all these superpowers, but he's always too busy fighting the latest bad guy to ever do anything practically positive with these powers.

As soon as SuperMan has overcome one enemy, the next one pops up and so it goes round and round, and there is never a time when SuperMan could actually use his powers for good, to drain a swamp, or to make a giant net that will drag all the plastics out of the oceans.

The direct result of the conceptual absence of the good side of the energy chart causes this crazy wall at ZERO.

Trapped on the negative side, everyone is circling round and round and round, repeating the old over and over and over again with no way out, no progress in sight.

It's worse than no progress as well.

The longer it goes on, the more destructive the absence of the positive side becomes on those poor energy bodies, trapped on the wrong side behind the ZERO barrier.

The Scientologists

A great example on how this works with real people is that of the Scientologists who took the Freudian idea that we are basically perfect but then were messed up by trauma entirely seriously and ran with it.

The idea is that if we remove all the trauma, we become clear of it, we become "clear."

So they would find people who were highly stressed, around -5 or -6, and gave them some focused attention and hope.

This would produce gains – the person would move up on the energy chart and start to feel a little bit better.

That proves the theory, right?

So all we have to do now is go on clearing trauma, and at the end, when there is no trauma left, we will have superhuman abilities, we'll never get sick ever again, and become the masters of the Universe.

So the Scientologists went at it and cleared their trauma – only, they didn't really clear anything because all they were looking for was that the E Meter would show ZERO.

ZERO for the energy body is exactly that – nothing. In order to heal or evolve the energy body, you need positive readings, but in that crazy world where everything stops at ZERO, that idea doesn't even exist.

More and more traumas were being taken to ZERO.

The gains started to flatten out, until there were no more gains at all.

At which point someone might have had the bright idea to ask, "Wait a minute – is there something else beyond clearing trauma to ZERO? Something beyond ZERO?"

Nobody did.

So they decided there had to have been more trauma, only perhaps it wasn't the trauma we remembered, but instead, trauma we didn't remember.

That opened up a whole new real of trauma clearance, but the gains didn't materialise.

Ah! Perhaps it is pre-natal trauma …

Same story.

Ah! Perhaps it is past life trauma …

Now we're starting to get crazy. Instead of further gains, people are starting to get strange new symptoms, getting ever more stressed, getting ill, acting strangely, definitely thinking very strange thoughts …

Where is the trauma???

Ah! Brilliant idea! It's alternate life trauma! And this could also include alternate past lives as well as alternate future lives … and now it's endless …

Trapped behind that ZERO barrier, with no way out, with nobody saying, "For the love of God, stop it with the trauma!" things were only going to get crazier and crazier.

Let me say this clearly and succinctly.

Trauma is not what shapes our lives. It is but a minute component and to start to look beyond trauma is what is desperately needed today to save us all from the crazy, dangerous stress overload we find ourselves in.

The Fish Tank Of Insanity

Running up against the conceptual ZERO barrier and cycling round and round between nothing and trauma, nothing and war, between nothing and misery, between nothing and decay, has created what I call the fish tank of insanity.

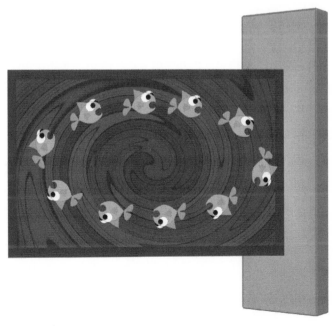

What is so crazy about this fish tank of insanity is that it is an entirely conceptual prison – it doesn't exist outside the minds of men who have lost the plot and the entire positive side of the Energy Chart.

There is nothing truthful or logical about the fish tank of insanity.

The real truth is that people experience positive emotions as well and all the time.

The world doesn't stop at ZERO – the real word, that would be.

The real world includes highs and lows and everything in between.

The real world, and especially the Oceans of Energy, is endlessly abundant.

Free The Fish!

As a Modern Energist, I hold it to be my purpose and mission to punch through that ZERO barrier so that …

The fish can swim free!

Choose Your Plane ...

Now I would personally like to free humanity from the crazy stress riddled fish tank of insanity all at once, but for now, I would be happy if individuals understood that there is a choice to be made, and then go ahead and make that choice.

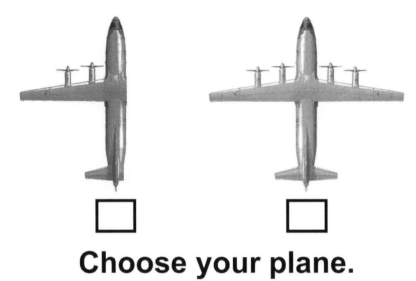

Choose your plane.

At the moment, people don't realise that there is this whole other world out there that holds the answers not only to almost all of their problems, but also to almost all of their life long questions.

At the moment, people don't even realise that there is a choice to be made – to go with the old or to take a leap of faith and embrace the new.

At the moment, every psychology session delves only into trauma and negative emotions and the past.

At the moment, every stress program drives people deeper into stress.

At the moment, the only answer to crime is deemed to be punishment.

At the moment, people are endlessly separated from each other by stress and have literally lost access to the source of their own personal power.

Disconnection

The more stressed and energy poor the energy body becomes, the more weak and fragile it becomes in turn.

This is a catastrophe in its own right with many terrible repercussions, but it does one more deeply fundamental thing that precludes people from working together to find solutions for our global problems.

The more stress there is, the more disconnected individuals become from one another.

I have likened what happens to the human energy body under chronic stress to what happens when you put a tree into a very small pot and cut off its roots and branches.

Not only does this lead to a severe shrinking of the entire energy system, and what we end up with is nothing at all like the natural order of things.

Where there could have been a mighty tree, we have an impoverished version that isn't even a shadow of what it should have been.

What also happens is that every little bonsai tree is all alone in its little pot.

In the real world, where the trees go large and to the light, their leaves touch each other, their roots form connections and the trees are not alone.

We often talk about potential and wonder how far we humans can truly go.

We wonder how to activate and actualise our true potential.

Expanding our energy systems, setting our energy bodies free to grow and expand with proper energy nutrition is definitely a step in the right direction.

Finding Yourself

You find out who you really are at +10, and only at +10.

Anything else is an impoverished version of you, a stressed version.

Your true self as well as your true potential becomes revealed when the energy system reaches its true Even Flow – and that's not sitting in the lotus position, gazing at your own navel and dreaming of better days.

At +10, when our energy body works exactly the way it was designed to work in the first place, we find ourselves.

We find the truth about human beings, we become truly loving – and finally also, truly logical.

Logic at ZERO is ZERO logic!

The Undiscovered Country

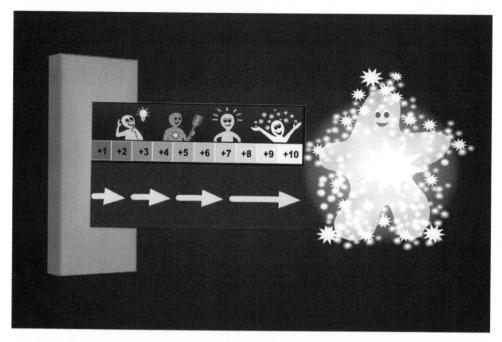

The most important message of Modern Energy is this.

To answer our most urgent questions, to solve our most urgent problems, but at the end of the day, to get out of that state of endless fire fighting, endless struggle and quite literally, the rat race in which humanity has been caught for far too long, we need to explore the positive wing of the Energy Chart.

Everything that is good, right, holy, logical, truthful, powerful and enlightening lies on the other side of the great ZERO barrier.

We need to start exploring what is going on in this totally undiscovered country of POSITIVE energy with all urgency and with all speed.

Everything Changes ...

The Power of the Positives has been ignored for far too long.

Understanding that literally everything changes when people become not emotionally balanced, but simply happier, is of the essence.

When our energy body states change, our entire body chemistry changes.

An aspect at -8 has a totally different body chemistry than a person who is at +8.

As a result, these different aspects (of the same person!) will react completely differently to all manner of physical substances.

Indeed, we would need to re-run every single medical experiment related to the effects of drugs on human beings because it was never factored in what energy body state the test subjects were in.

Give a -8 person an aspirin, and their reaction will be completely different from those of a +8 person. The very physical change in body chemistry that is the direct result of an energy body state change also gives us a myriad of new and promising research directions.

What does a +8 person have in their blood that a -8 person does not? And vice versa? There is so much that we must learn with great urgency to find better ways of treating not just the energy body, but also the physical body, as a direct result of factoring in energy at last.

In the meantime, each one of us has their own energy body, and their own energy body needs.

Every one of us can do simple things right now to start a true Renaissance of their energy body, and reap multiple benefits from doing so.

Each one of us can undertake their own journey of discovery, their own journey into the amazing land on the other side of that ZERO barrier, to find out new things about what we can do when we become more energy rich in our daily lives.

The Healing Energy Remedies

An entire lifetime of neglecting and not understanding the needs of the energy body has left us with all sorts of problems and in that constant state of fire fighting, circling around in our fish tank on the wrong side of ZERO.

Everyone needs urgent energy remedies and essential energy nutrition for the energy body, right now.

It is literally of the essence that we start to ask ourselves every day, "What I do I need? What do I want?" and finally listen and pay attention to the needs of our energy bodies.

We need to learn to be far more flexible in our approaches and ask often, pay attention all the time, and then actually use the extraordinary powers of positive energy to heal, rejuvenate and revitalise our energy bodies.

A huge part of The Love Challenge is to stop putting up with low energy states all the time.

We must stop to believe it is good to be stressed, that it is normal to worry and feel miserable, that it is right to be scared all the time, or that we have to suffer for whatever crazy reasons because it is good to be suffering.

All of that is of the old; it is understandable and a direct result of being trapped in those negative energy states, but it has to stop now.

We have to start picking up our power to take energy from the endlessly abundant, overflowing Oceans of Energy and use this to make ourselves happier.

We have to counteract the entrainments and habits of a lifetime and learn to ask ourselves all the time, "What do I need to be happier? Stronger? More playful? More joyful? How can I make my life more effortless, more beautiful, more exciting? What do I need right now to cheer up?"

When we have the answer, we need to not just nod and say, "Oh that makes sense ..."

We actually have to do something about it!

Modern Energy Tapping is a relatively quick and easy way to get started on providing our energy bodies with the energy nutrition they need to get stronger and grow up at last.

Modern Energy is not just tapping, however.

There are a myriad of ways we can gain better energy flow.

EMO Energy In Motion is natural and much faster; but simply learning to focus on uplifting and life giving energy exchanges in the real world is at the end of the day what drawing on the powers of the Positives is all about.

Aspects Of Love

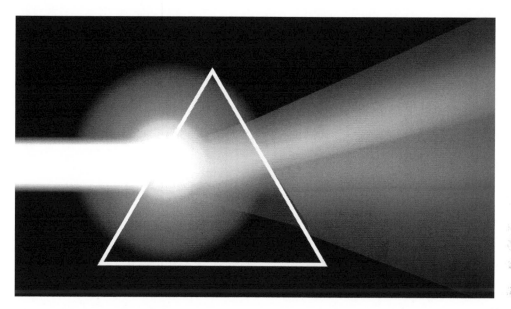

We have to remember that what we call the Positives are all aspects of love.

Love is the most powerful energy in the Universe, and it may well be so that our energy bodies are not ready to deal with that level of power.

That's alright.

We don't need to try and run the most powerful energy in the Universe through our energy bodies just yet.

We can simply start with aspects of love – the Positives, and indeed, the exact right Positives each one of us can feel we need, and hunger for, at any time, and anywhere.

Please note that this is not a Pollyanna approach to ignore problems or avoid dealing with problems.

We need to learn to ask, "What do I need to deal with this problem?" first.

We need to learn to empower ourselves before we delve into whatever problems we need to solve in our lives, because the solutions we come up with from the stressed states are no solutions at all.

They are not loving.

They are not logical. Stressed people simply end up creating ever more problems for themselves because they are in no fit state to be making good decisions.

When we are stronger, when we are on the right side of Zero, we start making better and better decisions and at +10, the solutions become revolutionary and truly astonishing.

Working with the aspects of love, the personal Positives, is the right thing to do.

The Healing Solution To The Problem Equation

The Positives are the right way to go.

Let me make this very clear.

It is not as though there was a choice between working with Positives, or focusing on the traumas, the old problems and the negatives.

It would be a choice if the outcomes were equal.

This is not so.

We do not arrive at the same place at all.

Working with Positives creates a positive outcome, every time.

It is the right way to go from fear to power, from anger to love, from defeat to victory, from failure to success.

As far as energy is concerned, simply adding the required energy (what we call a Positive) and then the next one, and the one after that, is how to get into higher energy states.

Keep adding energy, and a threshold shift occurs which transforms the energy body permanently.

It is simple, logical, correct and entirely predictable.

It is mathematical in its structural practicality. In other words, it works.

Expansion And Evolution

In the same way, as our energy system expands and we enter into the new territory on the positive side of ZERO, our understanding expands.

What was a little red heart that was the symbol of LOVE we go to the Heart of Gold, which expands more and more, until at +10, love becomes a flaring star.

This expansion is the direct effect of the higher energy states.

We understand more, we can handle more power, we have a chance to get to the truth of many things that seemed to be so mysterious.

Above all else, in the higher energy states we have energy enough to start giving, start loving in a whole new way.

Learning How To Love

You cannot love yourself – but you can love your aspects.

Love is an outward bound energy. It flows forward, as all things do in the natural Universe and trying to turn it back upon "yourself" causes chaos in the energy body.

Instead of doing that, we can start practising how to love our aspects.

We can start with the easy ones – the successful aspects, the happy aspects who did well.

We can think towards them and receive their energy, and send them our love and admiration in return.

I encourage you to try this; it is one thing to speak of such things in theory, and quite another to have the experience of improved energy flow when you connect with your aspects.

Once you have learned how to do this, you can send Positives to aspects who are still in dire need of energy help across time and space. Let your heart go out to those aspects and give them what they need, then go beyond and into love to raise them and transform them.

When you are ready, connect with those aspects that you are uncomfortable with or wish had never come into being.

All aspects need love to transform.

The more we practise our loving, the better we become.

The more we have, the more we have to give.

Please understand that our ability to love is not like a bucket that will run out.

Loving in the sense of sending energy to those who need it creates a portal through which more and more love can flow. Eventually, we can love all aspects, even those who are not our own aspects. In loving, we generate the energy we need to have our energy bodies grow up, become strong, become adult, become powerful.

The Starry Future

High energy star experiences is what the energy body needs to heal and to evolve.

To have a strong, powerful energy body and experience a different way of life, even if there is no change at all in the strictly material circumstances, we need many, many more positive star experiences.

In the past, these star moments were rare, unpredictable, and deemed to be dependent on money, youth, physical prowess, good looks, being particularly lucky, or relegated to special occasions, such as annual holidays, festivals or getting married.

The older people were getting, the fewer the chances of high positive experiences seemed to become – and nothing could be further from the truth.

High positive experiences are literally at our own fingertips and have always been.

The Oceans of Energy are all around us – and all we have to do is to make a conscious decision to turn away from the negative, and move forward, towards the power of the Positives.

With simple Modern Energy Tapping, we can have a high positive energy experience five times a day.

This will completely transform the way you act, think, feel and behave in under a month.

It soon becomes clear that you don't have to tap all the time to have high positive energy experiences.

Once we unlock the Power of the Positives, we realise that invitations to have high positive energy experiences are all around us, all the time – we were just too stressed to notice.

We didn't know just how much our own happiness matters to everyone.

We didn't think consciously about the importance of adding high energy events to our timelines all the time, every day, every night.

Now we do know. Now, it really is up to us whether we want to take up "The Love Challenge" and start seriously moving into a future that has a thousand times more star experiences than before. This is in our own hands, quite literally.

Plus Ten Is The Only Goal

Make it your own personal goal to find out who you really are when you get energy richer, when you shift your average energy state over time.

Don't be afraid of the many lies that were told about what happens on the positive side of the energy chart.

We don't turn into idiots here who don't understand problems. We don't run around like demented rabbits on steroids, and we don't strip our clothes off and wander the Earth with our rice bowls.

It is true that we don't really know what happens when we get to be higher, but chances are, we are going to be extremely surprised – and amazed, and delighted.

With the power of the Positives, we get to find our own journeys, our own way, each one of us.

We each build our own unfolding path with each step stone of high positive experiences.

Now that we know this is good, and right, and so very necessary, we can begin our own personal journey of discovery into the unknown world that awaits on the other side of ZERO.

Everything Works Better With Energy!

Modern Energy is all about taking the energy body seriously and helping it to heal and to evolve.

When we factor in the energy body, *everything* changes.

We can find new ways to solve old problems.

We can do things that are real and have real results.

Above all else, once we step out of the old mindset that keeps humans trapped in the fish tank of insanity on the wrong side of ZERO, we step into a whole new world of possibility, a whole new world where love is no longer just a word.

Now, it's over to you.

The journey is beginning.

Choose your plane ...

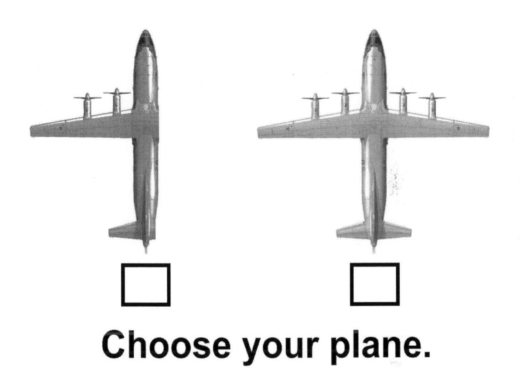

Choose your plane.

About The Guild Of Energists

In 1998, Silvia Hartmann created the first Modern Energy organisation to teach the first generation of directly energy based treatment techniques which became The Guild of Energists as we know it today.

No longer a sub-set of the other fields in the Mind, Body, Spirit triad, Modern Energy is The Third Field and Modern Energy professionals specialise in treating the real, living human energy body.

Modern Energy Tapping is a simple introduction, self help and therapeutic Third Field method.

- **The Guild of Energists provides education in Modern Energy and welcomes everyone who loves energy.**

Modern Energy knowledge is of the essence to help people make sense of their lives, to heal from emotional/energetic wounds and disturbances, and provides sound theory and practice.

GoE Modern Energy Trainers are transforming the lives of real people worldwide.

Quality Trainings In Modern Energy

Experience the power of Modern Energy by taking part in GoE's extraordinary, wonderful courses, for individuals and helping professionals anywhere in the world today.

Modern Stress Management Foundation

Find out how stress has affected your life, learn how to measure your stress levels and experience four outstanding techniques to raise energy. A brilliant, life changing course for everyone.

Modern Stress Management Professional

Discover Modern Energy techniques to work with individuals, groups and corporations to dramatically reduce stress and in turn increase happiness, motivation and creativity.

Modern Energy Tapping Foundation

Discover the joy of Modern Energy – literally learn how to tap into the Oceans of Energy! Learn how to solve problems, how to energy tap with friends, family, groups and children in this exciting course full of awesome exercises and experiences.

Modern Energy Tapping Professional

Working as a professional Modern Energist, learn to address the energy component in presenting problems and help people's energy bodies heal and grow strong. This is a truly groundbreaking course, utilising the Powers of the Positives to help the Modern Energy Professional become more powerful, more confident, more healing.

EMO Energy In Motion Master Practitioner

Beyond simple energy tapping lies a whole world of energy in motion. This course is particularly designed to develop the true 6th Sense and work with energy in real time, including conversational energy work. This course makes the Modern Energist.

Modern Energy Healing

The human energy body is real, it is not subtle in any way, and with Modern Energy theory and practice, we can put an end to the nonsense of the past and create real healing events through laying on of hands, the Royal Touch and more. This is a life changing course for people who know they have healing hands.

Modern Energy Coach

Become a one-to-one Modern Energy Coach and help keep your clients on track to work towards and achieve their dreams.

Modern Energy Dating Coach

Become a specialist in helping people with their love lives by reconnecting them to their 1st Circuitry.

SuperMind Master

Modern Energy ends the crazy confusion about unlocking the powers of the Energy Mind. Previously known as the sub- or unconscious mind, the Energy Mind is the most extraordinary information processing system and of the essence to be able to read and write energy.

Modern Energy Trainer

The Guild of Energists organises a seven day intensive teacher training course each year. You'll be taught how to teach a wide range of Modern Energy courses to your students, either by live training, one-to-one coaching or by distance learning.

Further Information

Join The Guild of Energists!

If you love real energy, and you want to learn more about Modern Energy and what it can do for you, join The Guild of Energists.

We are a vibrant community of people of all ages from around the World who have one thing in common – we LOVE energy!

GoE.ac/Join

The GoE Energy Conference

Each year, Modern Energists from around the world gather in the UK for an energy experience like no other! Take part in fun filled, experiential workshops, find Modern Energy Art, books, information and energy artefacts, get a fabulous conference manual and goodie bag with surprises, but most of all, meet amazing people who have lots of love to give.

GoE.ac/Conference

The GoE On Social Media

The GoE's official Facebook page:

Facebook.com/GuildOfEnergists

The GoE has members groups for general members, professional Modern Energists and Modern Energy Trainers.

For all latest news, events, practitioner listings and the member's library please go to:

GoE.ac

Books & E-books

Modern Energy Tapping – Silvia Hartmann

Start Unlocking The Power of the Positives in your life today!

DragonRising.com/MET

EMO Energy In Motion – Silvia Hartmann

The theory and practice of Modern Energy

DragonRising.com/store/EMO/

Infinite Creativity

The story of Modern Energy, Project Sanctuary, The Energy Symbols, Energy Events, Modern Energy Art told by Silvia Hartmann in her own words.

DragonRising.com/store/infinite_creativity/

The Energy of Attraction – Alex Kent

Applying the power of Modern Energy to Love, Dating and Relationships

DragonRising.com/EOA

About The Author

Silvia Hartmann is the creator of Modern Energy and the President of The Guild of Energists.

Creating a logical structure to explain human experience is her life's work.

Silvia Hartmann's favourite quote is:

"Love without logic is insanity. And vice versa."